PLAYING LIVE

Jez Rogers

For The Padawans -
Tony, Dan, Jason, Dave, John, Ben for making this necessary,
and for Rolo & Phil for making things work,
with my thanks

© Jez Rogers 2012
ISBN 978-1-4717-8208-4

This edition 2012

Contents

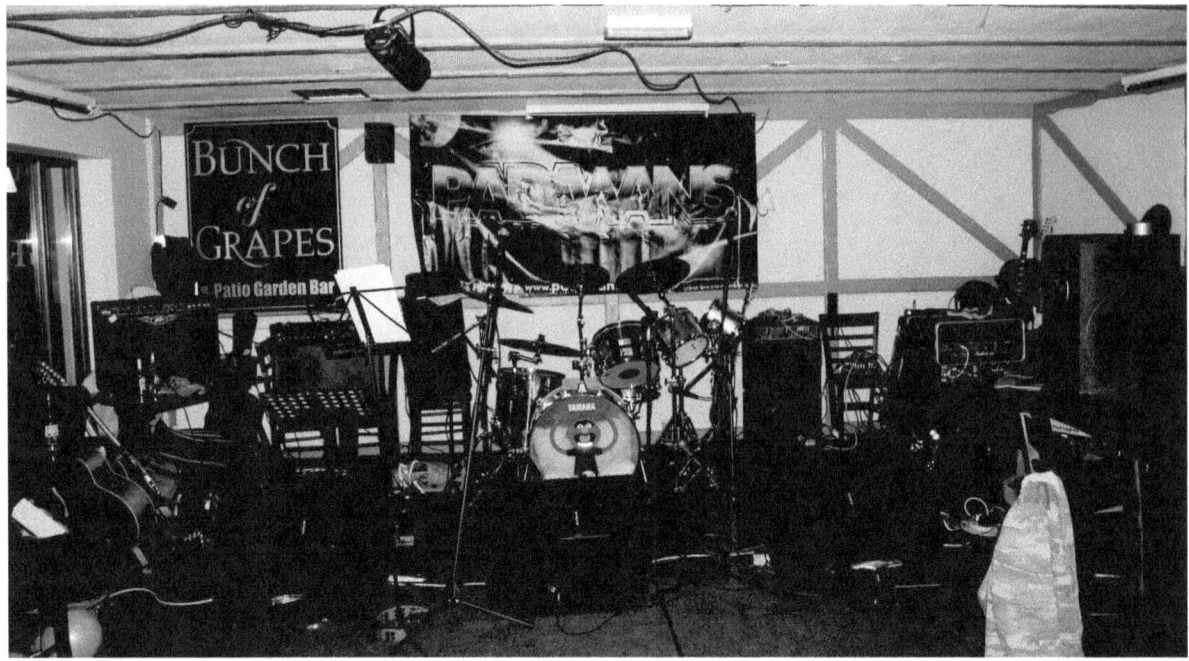

This book is for people starting up a band and looking to go from garage/practice room to real venues. It will also help solo artists and small combos making the leap from playing at home to playing in front of an audience. A book that explains what you need and why you need it, and also how it works - but not what you should actually do with it, I'd never presume to dictate that, its one of the real joys of rock and roll. Expect to learn everything about putting together a back line and getting the sound you make to the audience - you'll understand the whys and hows of using monitors, PA, mixers and power amps not just individually but as one machine that produces your live sound. It can't help but get technical at times but take it in comfortable bites - learn what you need and practice it as you go. Once you've factored in your own disasters and mistakes you'll be a master. I wish I could guarantee you no disasters and mistakes but it's the only way any of us really learn anything - however, as a band, we made every mistake you can imagine - and a lot that you can't begin to - and that's a lot of mistakes that this book will save you from. You'll manage a few, regardless and no doubt come up with some all your own invention - I'd love to hear about these so do keep in touch! The greatest pleasure is in knowing that there are people reading and using this book on their way to becoming famous live acts - Enjoy the trip!

Welcome to an experience that's amongst the greatest fun things you can do with your clothes on (although that's optional, I guess...). It is, however, also a prime source of arguments, fights and massive sulks! This book is dedicated to those who want to be right - and able to prove it!

Your Sound

A reasonably obvious starting point is to be clear about just what sound it is that you want to project to your audience. Fuzzed up grunge, clean and country, industrial rock, psych rock, sleazy blues, indie... the range of overall sounds a band can produce is incredibly varied, even when there is just three to five of you with basic gear. You do not have to settle on just one type of sound to make things easy – a lot of the gear you'll have sells itself on versatility these days, on the ability to model and emulate a wide range of ' classic sounds' – just be aware that switching from one to another for a full band in a noisy venue is a tad trickier than simply changing a pre-set in your bedroom. Bear in mind too that changes which involve foot switches and stored settings might be straightforward when you're playing at home but on a crowded and unfamiliar stage with dim lighting and the urgency of the moment, things can go horribly wrong.

One of our earliest gigs saw the introduction of the lead guitarists new amp – 100w of mega-modelling that could switch him from bright sunny reggae to chugging Sabbath darkness with one press of the foot switch, not to mention a half dozen other soundscapes. What could go wrong? First, the bass player walked through the lead and unplugged the foot switch. Second, aside from a ghastly squeal when the foot switch was reconnected, the guitarist mixed up which toggle was which, cycling through a half dozen very different settings instead of smoothly switching to one. Third, the 'right' setting turned out to have been saved after a few beers in the rehearsal room and was somewhere beyond 11... The amp was retired from stage duty and replaced by a simple two channel valve combo, enhanced by a couple of simple effects pedals.

When starting out, aim for simplicity both in your sound and in your gear. You don't really develop your own sound until you've played a bunch of gigs, for one thing, and another lesson quickly learned is that what works – or seems to work – in the practice room doesn't always translate to a real venue. Early on we worked out a dramatic opener involving a dark stage and the band starting quiet before kicking in loud with the stage lighting – far too much could go wrong, and did. The audience thought there were power problems and were, in any event, busy talking amongst themselves, unconcerned with the 'dramatic intro' being staged for their benefit until the singer fell off the stage in the darkness, croaking the opening vocal from beneath a table as the lights blazed up when they all roared with laughter, not the intended outcome at all.

Solo performers can make problems for themselves too. Singing and playing is never easy to pull off so avoid the delights of fx and, especially, loop stations, until you can comfortably add them to your repertoire. Even the most basic of things, amplifying an acoustic guitar, needs a lot of thought. Some pick-ups lose the woody tones, the ones that don't can over amplify guitar handling noises and feedback is an ever present problem that varies from venue to venue. As often as not, recreating the sound you are used to in practice can be a daunting task.

All newbie performers and bands soon discover that small venues that pack out absorb lots of sound whilst also making a lot of noise themselves and simply turning up the volume doesn't always work. The pub crowd isn't necessarily there to hear you play – you just happen to be on while they're catching up on gossip. Don't see this as a challenge, just do what you do and if it's good they'll start to take notice soon enough, especially if you've paid attention to the sound. Being loud isn't the answer and it doesn't mean 'rock!' – you have to be aware of how many different things need to be turned up, and of the balance that needs to be maintained between them. Finding that balance in the first place is where we need to begin.

"Go Loud!" - Live Sound

When a local band sounds bad its most often because they're playing too loud. 'Loudness wars' are a sure sign of inexperience – the drummer might kick it off, playing too hard and taking the bass with him, causing the guitarist to turn up his amp which leads the drummer to hit harder whilst the vocalist, trying to be heard, is just a hoarse scream.

Your singer will only be able to sing in tune if he can hear what he is singing. Your guitarists will only bend notes accurately if they can hear their own guitars. Bass and drums will only lock in if they can hear each other, and each of you will only know where you are in a song if you can hear the rest of the band. On-stage is wholly different to the confines of the garage or practice space and this can really throw you all. You will be struggling to hear the overall sound and may even have trouble in properly hearing your part of it. What you need is 'foldback' – to hear the overall sound that you are producing. At least the vocals need to be relayed through speakers called 'monitors' - no matter how good you all are as musicians, no matter how much you've practised, without good monitoring you will end up out of time, out of tune and wishing you'd stayed at home. When the on-stage sound is wrong, amplifying it will just tell the audience how wrong it is.

Bands tend to obsess about how much volume is being delivered to the audience but clarity and definition are far more important and the key element to getting things right is the foldback, the onstage sound.

The Essential Elements

Here's what your live sound comprises:-

1) **The Backline** – This includes your guitar and bass amps, and your drummer.
    2) **Monitors** – these are on-stage speakers relaying "fold-back" – your own sound
    3) **PA** – the front of house sound which the audience hears

The Backline

You will need **30 to 50watts RMS** for your guitar to match the drums. Larger venues may need a beefier amp but good quality guitar amps can be mic'd and put through the desk where the volume is balanced so you don't need a massive stack. I've lugged a hefty 100w valve combo around many smaller venues and it's never been turned up above 4. There is, though, a good point to be made concerning 'headroom' – consider car engines, for an analogy: there isn't a massive difference in the top speed you can get from a one and a half litre engine compared with a two litre engine, the difference is more a matter of *power*. The bigger engine will be comfortable at 70 mph while the smaller will be making more of an effort, Pushing amps is very similar to this, smaller ones turned up will be pushed to distortion while bigger ones still have power is hand – *headroom*. You'll hear this term a lot from sound engineers – it also applies to setting the gain trim on a mixer, for example. Back to our amp analogy, at small gig levels you aren't likely to be needing more than a comfortable saloon, turbo-charged roadsters can come later – but then again, a micro compact is likely to be underpowered for the job. Bear in mind that valve amps have the capacity to give you lots of headroom at much lower wattage.

The bass will need **50 to 100 watts RMS**.

House PA's don't often include spare microphones (if any at all) so it's as well for the guitar and bass players to invest in their own or there will be a need to borrow or hire kit.

If you are using keyboards they will need **100 watts** *as a back-line instrument*– but you can choose to put the keyboards directly through the PA to the front of house (bear in mind that *without a mixer* they will then be a distraction for the vocalist). This also covers the use of samplers.

Those pieces of kit which do not have a volume control – the drummer and the singer – now need to be considered. Vocals are a front of house issue but drums are decidedly back-line. You will need to decide whether or not the drums need to be mic'd up and, if so, whether to mic just the kick drum or the full kit. In small clubs, bars and pubs it's often more a case of getting the drums quiet enough rather than getting them loud enough. A drummer typically produces an output equivalent to a 400w amplifier so drum muffling is an essential art to master. If it is necessary to mic up the kit, it's often adequate to use just an overhead mic suspended from a boom stand – a condenser type mic is best. Sets of drum mic's can be bought or a bunch of dynamic instrument mic's used for the toms, snare, hi hat and cymbals. The drummer should consider having his own set of drum mic's, together with stands as a part of his kit where playing venues that need the drums mic'd is commonplace.

The vocals will definitely need a system that delivers over guitars, bass and drums to a room full of noise absorbing people (and audiences absorb the higher frequencies more efficiently than the lower ones), so PA's are first and foremost the province of the vocalist. They are also used for acoustic instruments and keyboards, and may be used to deliver a mix featuring the entire band, including drums.

Monitors

You need stage monitors so the singer can hear themselves and the rest of the band can hear the singer. A monitor is a speaker, often quite small and wedge shaped, which can be pointed at the singer without hiding him and generally raised at the front edge by a stand (or propped up by an old brick) to point at the recipient's head. Add more monitors so the rest of the band can hear the singer and position one of these next to the drummer. Large rigs – and stages - will also feature 'side fill monitors' which are pretty much self-describing. You'll need a separate power amplifier to drive the monitors although it needn't be as powerful as a PA power amp, and if you have extra acoustic instruments you will need to put these through the monitors too. Look for 'wedge' monitor speakers of at least 100W. You can get 'active' ones with *built in* power amplifiers or go for a power amp with separate 'passive' speakers. 'Active' monitors have their own amplification system, 'passive' monitors need a power amp to drive them.

We generally use a separate mixer for onstage sound which can be operated by a 'stage sound tech' - who is, as often as not, one of the band, adjusting levels and balance when needed. If you opt to run everything from a main mixing desk, also running the PA, you simply run the monitors as an auxiliary send, choosing the outputs you want to monitor and setting the level for the auxiliary 'mix' which you simply feed by cable to your monitor mixer.

Remember that your *backline* guitar and bass amps are on-stage monitors too. You need to set these so that you can hear yourself and the other band members, and that they can hear you as well as themselves. This is the trickiest part, especially when the backline isn't going through the main desk. When sound wars break out on stage, often a competition over being loudest, it's the audience that suffers. Don't make the mistake of turning up your amp to impress the audience as you will just be unbalancing the band's sound. Don't turn up – or down - your amp if going through the main desk, leave this to the sound engineer, it's his job. After a sound check you might find gaffer tape over your amp controls – it would be a lie to say that this isn't to deter you from fiddling but its actually to ensure that the optimum settings painstakingly worked out at sound check don't get changed. At a gig with several different bands – and backlines – my big valve amp, already 'sound-checked'. was once lifted back into place for our set by two stage hands who, in the process, nudged the overdrive channel volume all the way up – not a pleasant surprise when I first stomped on the channel switch foot pedal - and just as disastrous had it gone the other way. If your gear is shifted after a sound check get the sound engineer to make sure nothing has changed, if possible.

PA

To the singer, the PA is what an amplifier is to a guitarist, but it's much more besides. What goes to the PA goes through a mixer. These days a mixing desk capable of handling the whole band can be picked up for the price of a lower mid-range guitar and its well worth considering an investment in one along with power amps and speaker cabs rather than hiring in or borrowing kit for gigs where there is no house PA. Many venues, even smaller ones, now have their own PA systems, including a mixing desk, and you will need to come to terms with the use of these. A band playing pub gigs with mainly vocals through the PA will find just a few hundred watts per channel driven by a powered mixer to be a practical and affordable choice. At the most basic level if you only have vocals going through the PA you will only need 100W per channel and a couple of full range speakers with stands. The speakers will have a ten, twelve or fifteen inch bass speaker and a horn to handle the high notes. You'll need to *raise the horns above the audience* or the people at the front will absorb all of the treble and the rest of the room will get mush. This is why most PA systems feature stands, so use them!

Putting The Elements Together

The first step in getting your sound right (balancing your sound) is to get a clear mental map of how the sound process will actually function at your gig. In the practice room it's straightforward – you stand in a small room with your amps and your drummer and you make a noise, you can pretty much all hear everything since you are in a small space playing to each other – but now take that nucleus of noise and put it at one end of a small hall. Now fill the hall with a noisy crowd and ask yourself what they will hear – especially the folk at the back. To get some idea, walk out of the practice room while your band mates play full throttle, close the door, walk a few yards away, *then* listen. When you get a little distance from what seems like an epic rocking sound it all too often sounds like a confused and blurry mush. There won't be walls between the audience and the band at the gig but there might as well be.

In a venue, your amps and the drums form 'the backline', whilst vocals will be delivered to 'front of house' through microphones connected to a public address system, a PA, to be delivered throughout the hall. In a small venue, the backline will probably be able to fill the room without being turned up to maximum, though this will depend on the output of your amps. When practicing you'll have grown accustomed to *balancing your sound to the drums* but you'll need to be louder for your gigs. The answer is not to simply crank everything to 11. You now have control and balance issues to consider. Either you balance the back line *to the drummer* or you microphone the drums and *balance through the PA* .

If you are struggling to hear yourself don't get into a volume war with the other guitarist and/or bass player, it's the balance that is wrong. The drums, effectively, need to act as the volume control if the backline volume needs to be raised – maintain this balance. If the backline is too loud a number of issues arise. For one thing, you'll struggle to hear yourself clearly, never mind your band mates, but turn yourself down and no-one will hear you above the others. Keeping within sensible levels you can balance the volume of guitar/s and bass against drums, and keyboards if you have them. Each band member can move towards their back line kit to better hear what they are playing, and knows where to go to check the other guys too. The vocalist is the one band member who will not be able to hear himself without **monitors** – ie a system providing 'foldback sound' that allows him to hear what he is singing.

Ideally you'll already have worked with a small PA for your vocals, perhaps through a simple powered mixer and this will have taught you the need to allow some space – maybe you've noticed the tendency for percussion and vocals to clash, for example. For another example, backline sound will 'leak' into vocal mic's and then you'll simply be producing noise which sounds 'mushy' and ill-defined. Finally, the vocals are being delivered forwards, not into the ears of the musicians – or the singer - giving huge problems with pace and pitch. Not only do you need to balance drums, bass and guitars, plus any other instruments in the mix, both with each other and with vocals, but you need to deliver this balance to the entire auditorium, and to deliver with pace and pitch on the mark each member of the band needs to hear what they are playing, what the rest of the band is playing and what the vocalist is singing. The vocalist, with the band behind him, will hear the backline but needs to hear himself. The audience needs to hear the balanced overall sound.

In venues with large PAs, although the full band sound for the audience is balanced by the engineer, the volume of the different instruments on stage still makes a huge difference. Drums will pick up in the vocal mic so a loud drummer can still drown out a quiet singer. Even with a professional foldback system, you need to work with the engineer to get a good stage balance. Aim to have as little as possible going through the monitors as it'll keep the sound clear. Just the vocals would be ideal. Control your levels on stage and position amplifiers to help the engineer to help you. The better the sound on stage, the more you can relax and enjoy playing.

Monitors & Monitoring

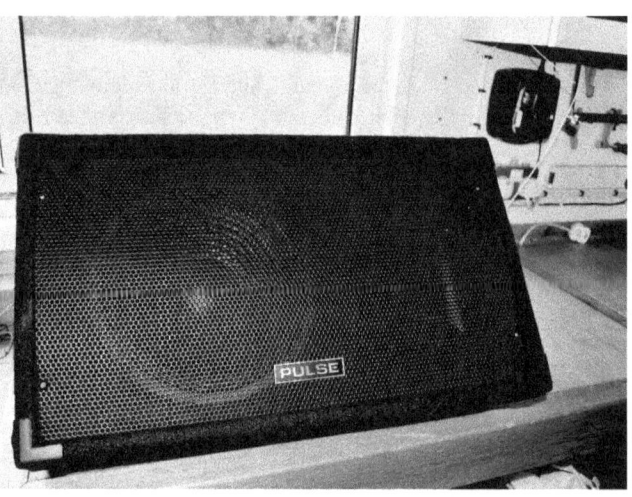

A stage monitoring system is a second PA system with the speakers directed at the performers providing what is often termed 'foldback' sound. At the basic level, all performers receive the same monitor mix whilst the most complex systems run from a dedicated monitor console offering individually tailored mixes. At the basic level, most mixers will allow the sound engineer to choose which channels – for example: choosing from vocals, guitar 1, guitar 2, bass, keyboards, backing vocals, drums – to route into an auxiliary output that feeds the monitor speakers.; to give each band member a different, individually tailored mix would require numerous outputs which only the most sophisticated high end gear will provide. At this level it is often the case that the monitors are 'in ear' by way of bespoke earpieces moulded individually to fit precisely. Audio engineering has progressed significantly since the late 60s when many bands played stadia without any monitoring at all. Unsurprisingly, there aren't too many live recordings of such gigs. The lack of monitors in the 60s doesn't mean that it's in any way desirable to go without – it was simply a case of technology not being applied at the time and not a case of deliberately doing without!

You need monitors because you need a sense of the overall sound for pace, pitch and timing. Vocalists are at a particular disadvantage as they will find it very hard to hear their own voices above the hefty wattage of backline amplification just behind them. It's no use putting the vocalist in front of the PA speakers delivering his amplified voice to the audience as the amplified vocals will feed into his vocal microphone and get re-amplified, setting up a horrendous feedback loop. It's not just the guitars that the vocalist is struggling to hear, and sing, over - drummers deliver the equivalent of a 400w amplifier. As any singer soon learns, if you can't hear yourself sing its virtually impossible to keep perfectly in tune, and all too easy to be drastically off key. When it comes to the guitarists, bass and drums however, they do have their own monitoring right on the spot – the backline itself: amps and drums, but may still struggle to hear each other clearly, or to distinguish their contribution to the mix of sound.

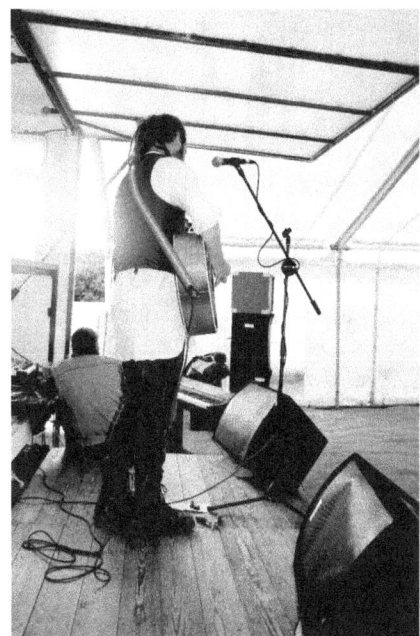

Wedge monitors for a small acoustic gig.

This is why on-stage sound is so important, and why monitors are essential for vocal foldback.

Keeping to our first gig focus, you'll be looking to keep it on budget and without too much complication. The size and nature of small, first gig type venues helps to define what is needed. First of all, understand that the use of foldback sound increases the risk of feedback from sound 'leaking' back into vocal microphones. What this means is that positioning is everything and also that the style of speaker used for the foldback is also important, directing the sound at the performers as precisely as possible so that it can be clearly heard without contributing too much to feedback levels.

The need for delivering foldback to each member of the band with minimal feedback leakage led to the development of **the floor wedge (see photo above)**. If you haven't come across monitors before, once you know what this is you'll see it everywhere – live gigs, television performances – check the rehearsal room footage from programmes like American Idol, The Voice, and X Factor. They don't always wheel out the in-ear kit, and not everyone gets on with that – something that is also apparent from the talent shows these days where a lot of the 'pitchy' issues are down to monitors and a performers lack of familiarity with them – having them is one thing but you really need to practice with them and get used to how you hear yourself. For one thing, getting used to hearing the foldback volume – tuning into it – can take a while.

The floor wedge is designed to be at a performer's feet with it's tilted speaker assembly aimed at their head. If you use ordinary speaker cabinets as monitors you'll need to prop them at the right angle using something like a brick. You'll also need to work out the positioning of the monitor and any backline amps which might otherwise be in danger of feeding sound directly into them. The positioning of vocal microphones is also crucial – cardioid mics are least sensitive directly behind so need to have their rear end pointed directly at the monitor's speaker face, hence the 45 degree angle tilt you'll notice vocal mics are usually set at on their stands. This isn't quite the case with hypercardioid microphones - these need to be set at a 45 degree angle to the monitor face so are usually kept level and the monitor itself slightly offset (see the diagrams). Your microphone spec sheet will show the best positioning to find it's 'deaf' spot.

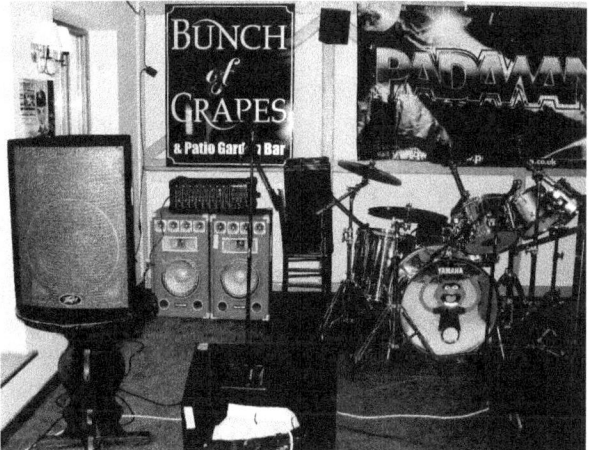

Wedge monitors in foreground, a small side-spill speaker set by the drums.

If there are feedback problems from monitors (*and see the full feature on dealing with feedback*) it will be due to positioning, as just described, so your sound check should highlight anything that needs to be positionally adjusted. If feedback occurs later band members should be aware that something may have been moved or turned up thus changing the dynamic – singers can wreak havoc when they play around with mics and mic stands just as guitarists can by turning up their amps during a set. Do it in the name of artistic expression and passionate performance by all means but do it with an awareness of the consequences!

If you have a mixer for your monitor system you may have a parametric equalizer which can be utilised to apply cut to troublesome frequencies. Once again, rehearsing with monitors will teach you just which frequencies can cause problems but the solution isn't as simple as it may appear. Simply 'notching out' – cutting – troublesome frequencies will often mean cutting the very sounds you want to be hearing – frequencies you need to suppress may only be a range of $1/20^{th}$ of an octave but using an equalizer fader could easily affect a whole octave. For this reason, sound checking needs to include 'ringing-out' the onstage monitors just as the main PA itself is always put through a 'ringing out' . See the full feature on The PA for how to go about this in detail but essentially it means increasing the gain gradually until 'ringing' starts (you'll know it when you hear it!) and then cutting offending frequency bands by just a few decibels. Monitor systems are likely to feedback at different frequencies to main PA rigs due to the positioning of the speakers so having separate equalisers is important. Larger PA systems often have a separate graphic equalizer for each monitor speaker that can be sent a feed. There are also now built in feedback eliminators with some modern systems in which the above process is largely automated. Not only do these set themselves up by identifying small, narrow problem frequency ranges as they appear, applying more cut to a number of bands without significantly affecting overall sound but they also provide filters capable of tackling 'unexpected' issues such as vocalists moving microphones during a set.

In very small venues it may be physically impossible to position floor wedges which can function properly as monitors. If there is some room it may be possible to manage with less floor wedges but it might be a better option to utilise a pair of small PA cabinets which can be placed on top of (or just behind) the main PA speakers. Point each one backwards at the opposite corner of the stage area. The resulting 'field of fire' should cover the entire band and as long as the foldback is dispersed by the distance from the back-line, sound reflection can be minimised. It's also possible to buy a purpose-designed small monitor that can be mounted on a mic stand close to the person using it – this option would suit bands likely to be playing small venues on a long term and regular basis and the large PA manufacturers have tailored solutions designed for this market.

Unless you have a very sophisticated mixer (that's the machine not the person – though I guess both could apply here), it won't be possible to 'tailor' individual monitor mixes so the sound engineer will need to mix band and vocals to an acceptable compromise mix that all share. In a small venue its usually the case that **only vocals** and any acoustic instruments and keyboards – all of which go through the PA system – are in the monitor mix. In other words, all those sounds that are routed directly to front of house and which are otherwise readily overpowered by guitars, bass and drums. The guitarists and bass player are parked in front of drums and amps so are effectively self-monitoring, with just the vocals (and any acoustic instruments) on the monitor speakers . The vocalist's monitoring comprises a mix of the backline stage sound just behind him and his own vocals in the foldback monitor.

In larger venues, the backline will probably need to go 'into the mix' in order to provide a balanced front-of-house sound. If in order to be heard at the back of the room, the backline needs to turn up to the level where band members can't hear each other speak at all - and at this level there will be feedback issues and the monitors won't be heard either – then the band needs to 'go through the desk'. A larger PA system is not simply more powerful but features bass, mid range and top range speakers, often with a 'cross-over' that splits the band's sound into three frequency ranges, each range powered by its own power amplifier. At this level, a sound engineer runs the mixing desk and has the ability to control the band's volume, delivering the level required by the venue without sacrificing sound balance and quality. It's possible to be 'quiet' on stage with the full band sound for the house controlled at the desk - mic'ing the backline (amplifiers and drums) reduces the amount of sound-spillage into vocal mics which also means a much clearer sound. In small venues with lightweight PAs designed for little more than lifting vocals over the backline sound of amps and drums, the balancing act is, perhaps, less complex but a lot harder to get right.

What you should by now appreciate is that you should, ideally, invest in your own mixer and monitors both to rehearse with and to provide monitoring at your 'starter-level' gigs. A simple powered mixer will manage the job and will happily drive three or four general purpose full-range 'wedge' speakers. Alternatively you could go for a power amp and speakers with a small, inexpensive mixer – effectively a 'mini PA'. For gigs, an 'aux send' feeds the monitor mix from the main desk to your monitor mixer.

The monitor mix

The monitor mix will comprise either just vocals, perhaps with any acoustic instruments, or the full band. Sometimes it may be desirable to put the bass through the desk. With the full band in the mix, guitar, bass, and drums will each have their own channels - drums may have a number of channels – separate ones for kick, toms, snare, cymbals, hi hats etc. How does the band get into this mix? Guitar amps can be mic'd using dynamic

Our checklist for live gigs has over 100 items on it... This is how a simple rig fits together:

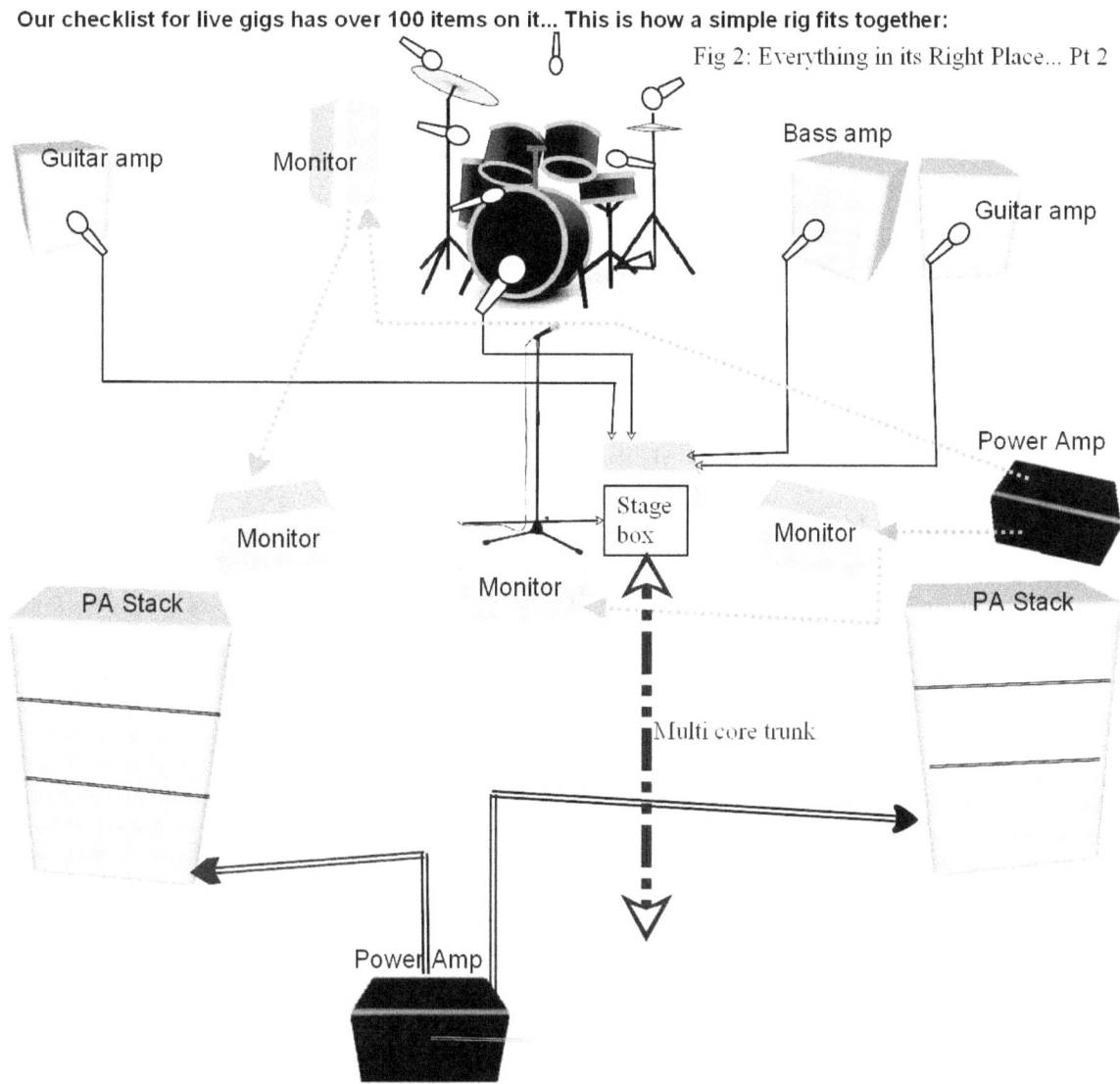

Fig 2: Everything in its Right Place... Pt 2

A simple stage plan for a basic band set-up.

instrument microphones such as Shure's SM57. Some guitar amps can be D I'd (DI stands for Direct Injection or Direct Input) directly to a mixer desk with a cable. Guitars, along with other instruments, can also be plugged directly into a desk by way of a DI Box which converts the signal from unbalanced to balanced – something we'll look at in detail later. You can use your monitor rig for practice sessions, monitoring at gigs and even as the sound system for small or 'unplugged' gigs. It's the best investment a new band can make.

Solo performers need to practice with a monitor too, getting used to how your voice will sound in a stage situation is important as some venues will project your vocal into a busy, noisy room and very little will come back at you. If you will be using backing tapes, drum machine or any of the new wave of iPad and iPhone gizmos for vocal and or guitar effects you're going to need to work out the electronic and acoustic set-up and practice it hard.

Practice using monitors and your band will become adept at playing tightly with minimal on-stage noise – don't be fooled into thinking this isn't 'rock and roll' – the best rock acts in the world play with a surprising lack of noise **on**-stage, even when delivering a huge front of house sound. If rock stars didn't work this way, most would be deaf! Bear in mind that the audience hears it maybe once in a couple of weeks, not 200 or more times a year.

Get Yourself Connected... How To Put It Together

Take the time to work out a stage plan. It doesn't have to precision drawn and correct to the last millimetre but it should serve as a diagram showing all the kit that needs to be arranged on stage and where on stage it needs to be. Keep it with an inventory of the band's gear – this should be detailed – list every cable and connector and identify the types, lengths and any other specifics. Whenever you can, recce venues first and have your stage plan and inventory with you. Look for the location of power points , check that they're functioning and safely earthed – simple, inexpensive testers are available from any hardware store and if you've ever taken an electric shock on stage you'll know how well worth it they are. Referring to your plan, note where each piece of gear is likely to go and how far it is from a power source. This way you'll be sure to have enough extension cabling (we use two cable reels with built in RCD trips) and multi-gang connectors with you. Consider too, the lengths of speaker cabling – for monitors, and the placement of monitors, also the lengths of cabling you'll need if mic'ing backline amplifiers and drums. Your recce can also help you decide whether or not you'll need to mic the backline and/or drums, especially if you go when someone else is playing. Lastly, your recce is also a good time to check out the house PA – Will you be able to put your backline through it, if it seems necessary? Will it feed to your monitor mixer and with what sort of connection? If you use a stage-box and multi-core cable to trunk to a mixing desk you'll be able, when you recce, to work out where the desk can go and how long the cable run will be. The venue may have its own stage box and multi-core – check the number and type of sends and returns it provides . Your recce should also help you figure out the best place to put the drums and if you're not sure, Ask! Where the drummer goes pretty much determines where everyone else will be so its key to your stage plan. Recording studios live rooms often have a drum throne bolted to the floor so newcomers don't have to go through the trial and error of finding out the percussion 'sweet spot' and even though small venues don't have much space for alternative locations there will likely be more variables involved than you'd imagine. We once had to set up in a skittle alley, the band virtually standing in a line, one in front of the other, drums at the back, to best project into an L shaped space studded with columns. Recce – you'll be glad you did.

Your own choice of monitors should include considering how they connect to the power amp/powered mixer, and to each other. Speakers can be connected with cables ending in 'speakon' type connectors, jack plugs or plain bare wire for winding onto posts. Often you can employ a mixture of these cable types and its essential to determine how you will connect speaker to speaker when you daisy chain in series or parallel. Be sure, also, that you use speaker cabling and not instrument cabling.

Stage Mic'ing

You may need to mic' up the back-line (and the back-line includes drums) so it's vital to know how to go about this. Further, setting vocal microphones isn't as straightforward as it may seem...

Vocal Mic'ing

The idea is to position a dynamic cardioid microphone as close to the singer as possible. The term 'vocal mic' doesn't relate to something that looks cool and lends itself to being swung around – it relates to the microphone's characteristics which will feature a 'presence peak' in the frequency response range which helps the singer's voice cut through. Taping the mic cable to the mic stand will help limit any vibration along the cable – leave a loop at the mic end for 'travel'. If the singer is prone to 'popping' – the effect of 'plosive' 'B' and 'P' sounds, or sibilant hissing, have them learn to back off slightly and to try singing over or under the mic – again, something learned in rehearsal and another reason for good fold-back. As described in the Dealing with Feedback section,

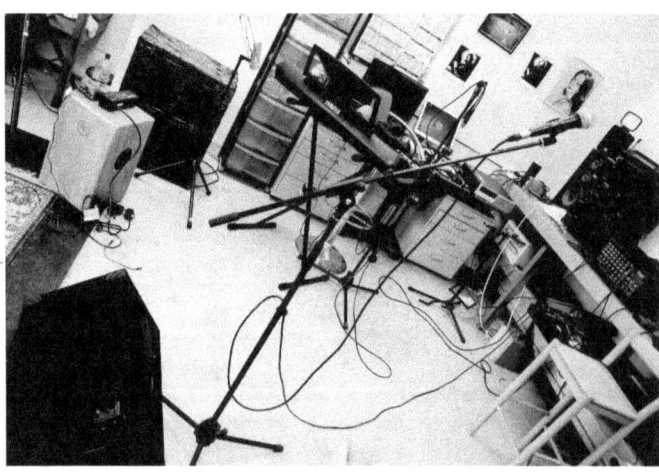

the mic should be pointed base directly towards the monitor, as in the photo above, (or at 45 degrees for a hyper-cardioid) to avoid feedback and the singer should avoid placing a hand over the foil of the mic head.

Electric Guitar, Mic'ing the Amp

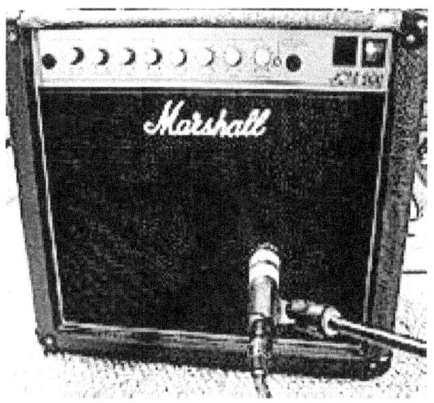

The crucial factor here is one of tone. It's possible to DI directly from amp to mixer, generally through a DI box but a guitarists sound is as much down to the amp as the guitar and the speaker setup of the amp is a key ingredient. By-pass that and you have a different tone to deal with. If the amp is nothing special, the guitarist may prefer a DI box solution that has a speaker emulation – giving a desired tone type, otherwise you will be mic'ing the guitar amp. The weapon of choice for this a Shure 57 – or an acceptable clone of this classic dynamic instrument mic. The mic needs to be as near the speaker grille as possible to avoid sound spill encroaching, the brightest sound will be obtained by pointing the mic directly at the speaker cone. Having the mic 'off-axis' will lead to mellower tones but if you simply suspend the mic by its lead so it's pointing at the floor you're not likely to get the best of results and will be inviting unwanted sound reflection from the floor surface. Use a small stand – guitar stands can be re-purposed as mic holders sometimes clamp on quite happily, purpose built ones are available though and boom-type vocal mic stands can also be used. Gaffer tape the lead to the deck once it's set, you don't want a careless foot sending it flying. Trial and error will soon tell you the best placement for the mic and its recommended you label the chosen mic. If you're mic'ing a twin (or more) speaker cab finding the guitar player's favorite sweet spot can take a while so marking the spot with colored tape is a good idea.

Bass Guitar, Mic'ing the Amp

Pretty much as for guitar amps but with the mic set back a few inches from the grille.

Acoustic Guitar, Mic'ing

A specialist acoustic amp can be mic'd, as for guitar amps above, but where an acoustic is used with a band it will generally be put through the desk via a DI box and using its own built-in pickup. If you do need to mic an acoustic guitar its often done with two mic's – one placed about 3 to 6 inches from the spot where the neck joins the body and the other placed further away to catch ambient sound – not an option if the guitarist is playing with a band. Condenser mic's will give brighter results. Moving the mic nearer to the sound hole will enhance bottom end. Modern, quality guitars have excellent onboard preamps and are designed to be played through sound systems – many now featuring balanced output lead options (3 pin XLR connectors rather than jacks).

Drums, Mic'ing & Muffling / Damping

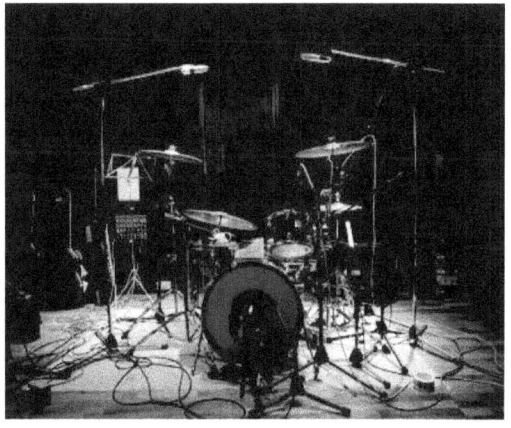

The purpose of mic'ing the drums, as with any other instrument, is to get a separate sound channel which can be processed as part of the overall sound mix - this enables you to give definition to the sound your drummer creates for the benefit of the audience beyond the PA system. If you are putting everything through the mixing desk you are almost certainly going to need to reinforce the sound of your drummer - or of his playing, anyway! We've acquired a huge array of microphones, mainly for the drums, and these let us rig for any eventualities. Small venues are rarely designed with rock music in mind - we've had fun with skittle alleys, L-Shaped rooms and all manner of either sound deadening or highly sound reflective surfaces. Often, you won't know until you set-up that there are problems. Always

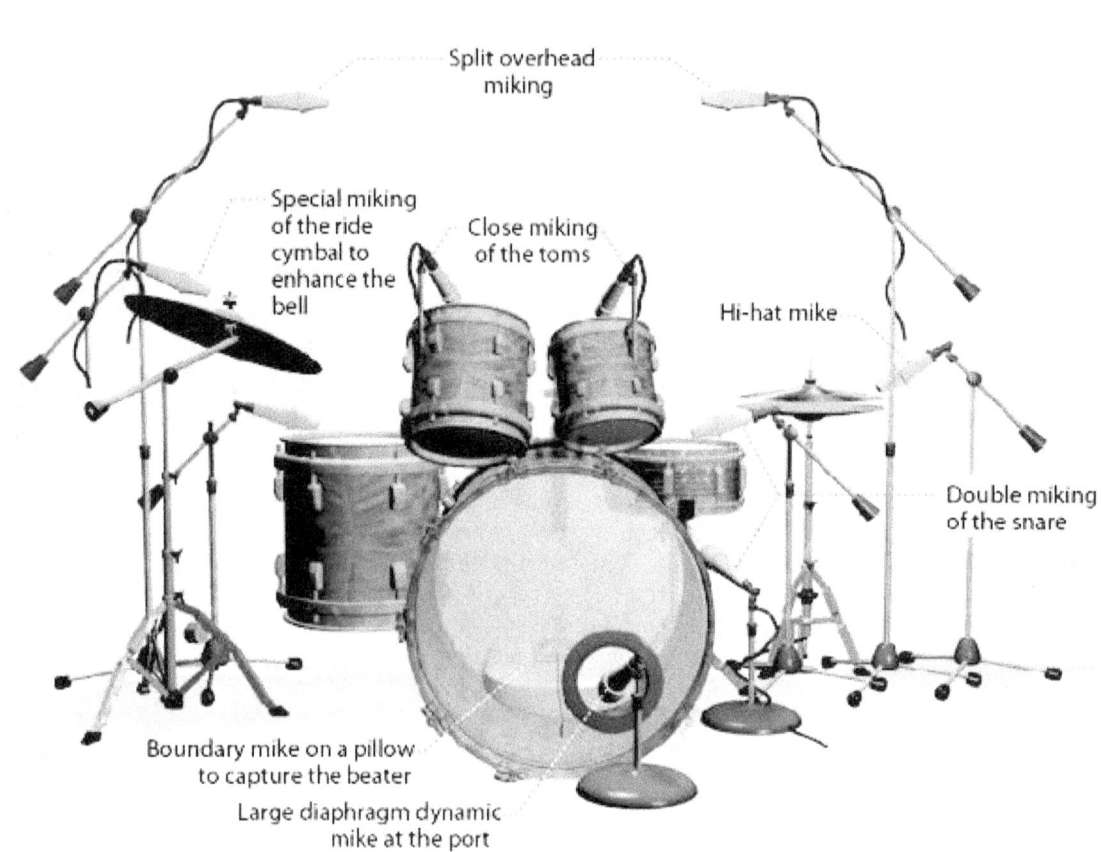

Split overhead
miking

Special miking
of the ride
cymbal to
enhance the
bell

Close miking
of the toms

Hi-hat mike

Double miking
of the snare

Boundary mike on a pillow
to capture the beater

Large diaphragm dynamic
mike at the port

travel with your own mat for the kit - never assume there'll be something there. As often as not, it's muffling that is needed in smaller venues but don't forget that the sound bouncing off the walls of the empty room can be quite different when the room is full of absorbent bodies.

Tuning the Drums

Preparation of the drum kit is the key to getting a good sound: First eliminate any rattles, clicks and buzzes. The drummer is usually the first band member to set-up for this very reason. The kick pedal is a prime source of such noises and should be securely attached to the shell. Oil and Blu-Tack will cope with most rattles and squeaks.

Check that the pitch is constant by tapping each drum skin around its perimeter. Double-headed toms are tuned to the same pitch. In practice sessions, try different tuning pitches on the bass drum as this can eliminate a lot of sound issues before you head for the live stage - this really should be a vital part of getting your band's sound right. Your drummer should have made the important decision about the hole in the front batter of his kick drum. The purpose of these is to add resonance and power - most skins now come pre-cut.

So set-up for resonance and power but be prepared to add muffling (see the detailed section below). Work in this order.

Listen for: When sound checking, both kick drum and snare must be heard to give clear, positive beats which decay before the next beat or a fuzzy and blurred sound will result. 'Black dot' drum skins give a better-defined beat - taping a beer mat at the point where the skin is struck gives a similar effect. A muddy effect can also occur on faster songs when beats are closer together - the tuning pitch determines the decay time for the drum sound, and it may be necessary to raise the tuning or to add damping to reduce resonance carrying from beat beat.

Tom-toms often have an excessive ring, but using their built-in dampers affects the tuning so alternative damping may be preferable (see below). The brightness of tom-toms often means that they won't need mic'ing.

Mic'ing Drums

A natural drum sound suitable for small combos, jazz work and similar can be obtained by setting up a stereo microphone pair a few feet in front of the kit and a few feet apart. For rock, additional close mics on the kick and snare will be needed, and possibly an ambient overhead – for which a condenser mic is a good option. Sets of drum mics can be bought and a committed drummer will certainly want his own as part of his kit. It will often be the case that a decision on whether the drums need to be mic'd won't be made until you're in the venue and know how the drums are likely to sound, so if the drummer has his own its a real bonus – otherwise spare instrument mics will need to be a part of your kit. I say how the drums are *likely* to sound – how they sound at sound check in an empty hall is different to how they'll sound in a hall packed with people. Better to err on the side of caution.

The kick drum mic is a dynamic cardioid with an enhanced bass response, but starter bands can manage with an ordinary instrument mic. The mic is placed inside the drum shell and pointed towards the spot where the beater strikes the skin. The mic for the bass drum (a dynamic, such as the Shure) allows the balance between the bass drum and the rest of the kit to be adjusted during the mixdown, letting the bass drum sound be treated separately. Led Zeppelin and The Beatles, used this setup to good effect and illustrate the range - power pop to rock that benefits from more than the simple overhead pick-up.

It is not necessary to mic every single drum: bass and snare are the powerhouse of the kit and the most important. The hi-hat bleeds through onto the other mics, leaving the cymbals to be picked up by your overhead microphone/s. The snare mic is placed about 2 inches above the drum and the same distance away from the edge, angled towards the center. The same applies to the toms but about 2 inches *in* from the edge rather than outside it.

A lot of leakage can spill from one mic to another, especially from snare and toms to the kick drum mic. Using noise gates can clean up drum sounds but a starter level, and bearing in mind that we are not trying to record an album, use a simple rule in which the distance from a mic to the drumhead is 'D' and that the distance between any two drum mics must be at least 3 x D.

Damping Drums

Damping is managed by taping folded tissue or cloth to the edge of the drum head or simply by getting creative with gaffer tape. The drummer should also be carrying a supply of 'moon gel' or similar – a sort of plastic putty that can be torn to size, adheres naturally and can be packed away in its tub afterward for reuse at the next venue (alternatively – try Blu-Tac, but it's no cheaper!). For the kick drum, use a woolen blanket and control the degree of damping by the extent to which the blanket is in contact with the rear head. Much of the need for damping is eliminated by having quality kit kept in good order – hence light on odd rattles. In smaller venues, simply mic'ing the kick drum is all that will be needed. Sometimes a simple two or three mic setup will suffice which is kick plus ambient/overheads. Experiment. As noted, overhead condenser mics capture drum sound really well and its generally easy to suspend a mic over the drummer and hope he doesn't swear overmuch at the bass player...

Setting Up Routine

The setting up routine begins back at base. Hopefully your band will feature at least one personality given to being something of a 'Quartermaster' – whether it's a band member or a friend who is happy to act as Road Manager, or maybe you have a Manager or your own Sound Engineer, someone needs to be in charge of the band's Load Out List including the organisation of all the kit listed on it. The Load Out List is an inventory of all the band's kit – everything needed for the gig. Use it as a check-list to see everything onto the van and then everything into the venue and set-up. When you load out of the venue use it again to ensure nothing is left behind. The list works better when all the kit is labelled – make sure, too, that the band's name is stenciled or labelled on kit, guitar cases with the player's name etc. Cables need labels identifying type and length – you can use coloured tape to distinguish between types and/or lengths for quick visual reference. Our Load Out List numbered everything and showed where each item was stowed so following the set-up plan you would find, for example, " *No 63 - XLR to Jack, 10m Multicore to Desk. Box 3*" and you'd find the 10m lead, with red tape indicating a 10m length, labelled *63 XLR/Jack Mcore-Desk,,* in Box 3 just when you needed it. To make things even easier we stow leads and cables in cardboard toilet roll inners, strengthened with gaffer tape. These make leads quick to spot, easy to label/re-label and prevent tangling whilst being stored, loaded and shifted around. When you see how long the Load Out List is you appreciate how necessary this is. The first time we set-up with this method, we set-up a full hour faster than previously and got progressively quicker every time afterwards. Make a list of each job that needs to be done, and

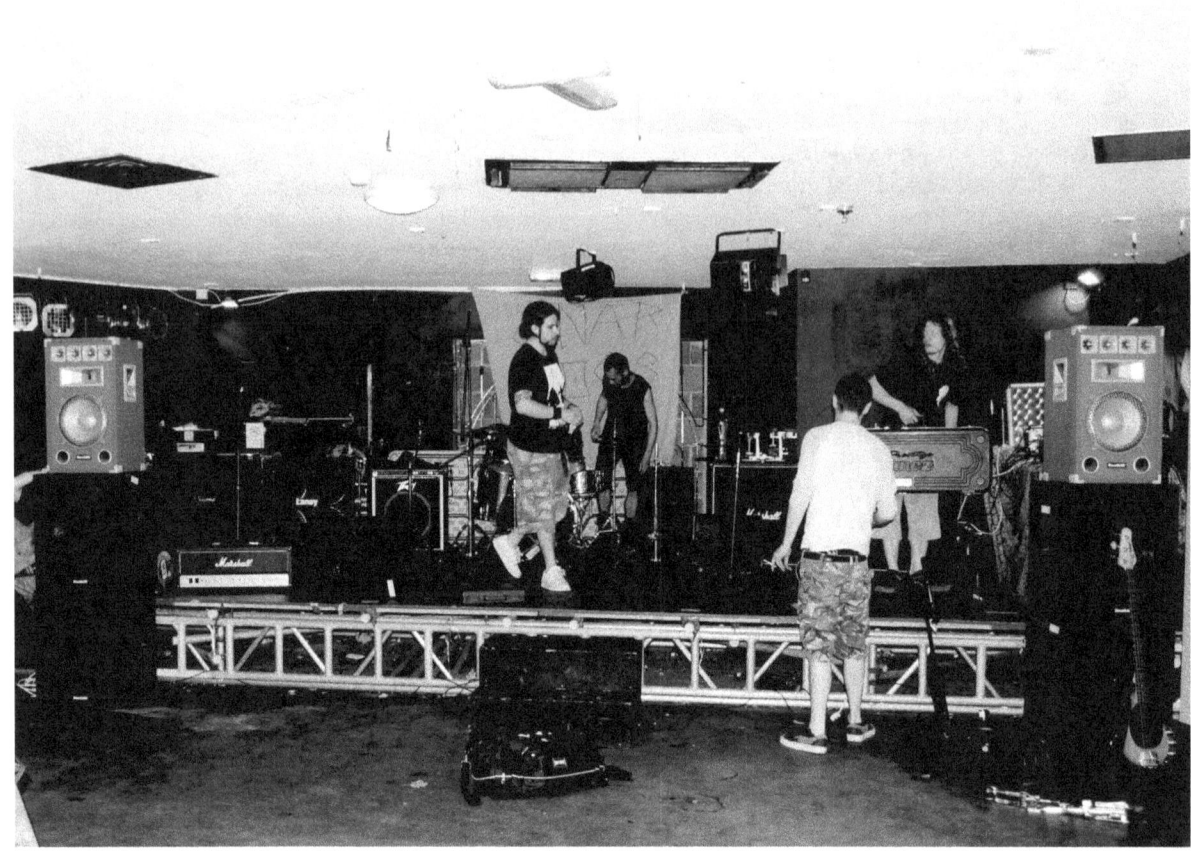

in what order – this is especially useful when there's four or five of you doing it, you'll load in and load out like clockwork and always know where everything is. "This lead is dud" – "What is it?" - "XLR, it's a DI from the bass cab, 10m" – "Spare 10m XLR/XLR in... box two" – "Got it". There's another message here, too – always have spares!

The advantages of this admittedly somewhat anal approach are that venues and their resident sound guys will love you, you'll be set-up very quickly with plenty of time for the sound check and if something goes wrong you'll readily know whether you've a spare or not and where it can be found. We even have guitar strings, picks, drumsticks, batteries and fuses on our load list. Never forget the batteries and fuses – though you only need them when you don't have them.

The following is a simplified set of instructions for getting a basic system up and running with as few problems as possible.

A Basic Stage Setup

• (1) Place the front monitors near the edge of the stage, aiming back at the performers.

• (2) Place the mics and stands in front of their respective monitors at a distance of 1 to 3 feet, depending on the cabinet's up-facing angle - the speakers should be aiming directly at the backs of the mics. Other monitors should be located as closely as possible to the performers, also aiming at the backs of their mics. This is to reduce feedback potential.

• (3) Place the main FOH (front-of-house) speakers at stage front at the far corners aiming straight out at the audience. Do not aim them in at the audience in front of centre stage unless the stage is deep enough for the mics to be set farther back to reduce feedback.

Connections :

• (1) Connect all mics, line-level signal sources - i.e., tape decks, CD players, instrument amp line outputs, etc.- also processors and external effects units, to their respective channel inputs or send and return jacks on the mixer (for more information see INPUTS and OUTPUTS under THE MIXER).
It is a good idea to identify the various channel sources, perhaps with small stick-on labels at the bottoms of the channels, e.g., "lead vocal", "guitar", "drum vocal", etc.}
• (2) Do not connect speakers yet. Transients from things being plugged into the mixer and switched on can cause speaker damage eventually if not immediately. Connect speakers last.
• (3) Similarly, when you are connecting one or more external power amplifiers and speakers, be sure to connect the speakers to the power amp after it has been connected to the mixer and the mixer has been powered up. The reason for this is because some mixers do not have turn-on transient suppression built in. Any power amp(s) which are connected to the mixer and running with their speakers connected when the mixer is switched on can amplify this large burst of signal voltage with a resounding "pop" or "boom" and the speaker system may be damaged. Even if the speakers survive this type of accident the first time, repeated accidents will eventually take their toll. *If there is a power failure during the job, try to switch off the power amps immediately, before the power comes on again. Mixers with built-in power amps usually don't suffer from "pop" problems when switched on, but it's not a bad idea to turn the master levels off before powering them up.}*
• (4) Electronic crossovers or speaker processors should be connected between the mixer and power amplifiers. The term "between" means mixer output to unit's input and unit's output to power amp's input/s.

Ringing Out the Monitor System

Finally, once you're set up you'll need to **ring out** your monitor system (if you are using a mixer with graphic equalization for your monitor system). With the system operational and all mics turned up to their performance settings (or a rough approximation of them) you can ring out the monitors. Ringing out applies to both the main PA system and the monitor system – the procedure is the same though it will likely be more precise and sophisticated for the PA. Start off with all the EQ faders flat, then increase the system gain until you start to get feedback. Back off the level until the system is just ringing when someone talks into a mic. Identify the frequency of the ring by pulling down the faders one at a time. Return each fader to the 0 position if nothing happens and go on to the next. Once you've found the fader that makes the ringing stop cut by about 3dB and then turn up the gain again until ringing starts. If it is at the same frequency apply a further 3dB of cut and continue. If the ringing is at a new frequency, pull that fader back by 3dB. Repeat the process until the worst ringing has been removed. You can only do so much before the overall sound begins to suffer and alterations no longer have any real effect but you'll have removed the sting and, with an audience in the feedback threshold will effectively be around 5dB higher. Now roll off the overall system level by about 5-6dB to restore stability. And leave yourself headroom.

Now check the monitor speakers working with your channel faders at about 75%. As the first frequencies to 'ring' tend to be those that provide clarity you might need to reduce the amount of cut a little for these or the sound may be dull and dead. Just 1dB less cut can make all the difference.

The Sound Check

The best way to get a good sound is to do as the sound engineer suggests. The sound engineer knows the venue and the PA. In general, the quieter the sound on stage the easier it is to get a good sound out front. If all that the singer can hear is your guitar, they won't have much chance of being in tune. And a flat singer means a flat gig. Bands need to understand the difference between *power* and *volume*. I've worked with major bands who have a huge sound out-front but are eerily quiet on stage. It's because they've worked hard to get the right basic sound. Just cranking your amp up doesn't make the sound more *powerful*, it just makes it *louder*. At a local level I constantly see bands slide into a high volume thrash that feels awesome in the adrenalin charged rehearsal room but is just a muddy mess for an audience that isn't a part of it. It really pays to book a larger practice space and rehearse with your own monitors and mixer, learning to balance your essential band sound. Once you have that you can export it through a mixer to be delivered to the audience at whatever volume is necessary. A mic'd AC30 can be cheerfully matched with a Marshall stack in a house mix – though at the same back line volume setting one will reach a lot

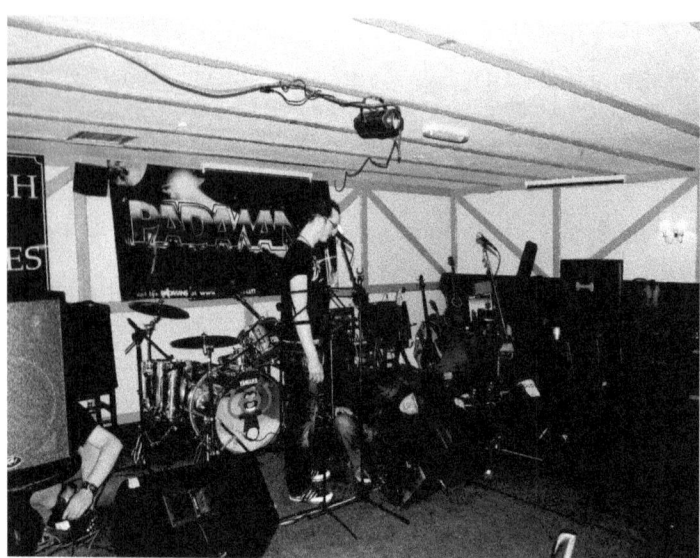

further than the other. In a small venue the audience often shares your on-stage sound, with just the vocals being carried by the PA and this is actually one of the hardest sound balances to get right so make sure you allow plenty of time for your Sound Check.

There is a *structure* to a Sound Check – or at least *there should be*. In the first place you need to set up, then set up your on-stage sound, lastly comes the PA, the sound that goes out to the house. Bear in mind that this does not allow for odd band members wandering in at the very last minute for 'their' sound check – you need the band together. You should already know whether or not anything other than vocals is going through the desk but be prepared for last minute changes of plan – the Sound Check is where your sound for the night is finalised. If it's just your band that's playing you should have plenty of time (provided you haven't left it until ten minutes before kick-off that is) but if there is more than one band on the bill be prepared to have just one song's worth of time after the headliners have set-up and checked. When you're sharing a stage set-up you may well have to live with a basic set-up created for all: if this is the case, it's a matter of familiarising yourselves with the on-stage conditions and negotiating whatever tweaks you feel are necessary – do ask, you have nothing to lose! There are many things a Sound Engineer can adjust within an overall shared set-up without any real difficulty – one example: A band with two guitarists sharing lead lines may need to have the two players separated in the mix, something the engineer can manage using the Pan control which can move individual instruments from the centre out to either 'side' of the audio mix.

If anything, the first ever sound check is more terrifying than the gig itself. You are suddenly confronted by people asking technical questions and speaking some strange hybrid language, all of whom regard you and your mates with a wary disdain as they run their eyes over your kit. Drummers, make sure you read up on drum muffling and mic'ing *(page xxx)*, guitar players, be sure that you know all the ins and outs of your amp set-up: Is there a line-out? Do you plan to use a separate 'clean/acoustic' amp? Do you use an FX loop? It's not a good time to decide it may be a good idea. Volume pedal? Do you have a list of the amp modelling effects you will be using? Ideally, you won't – not for your first gigs anyway. Once you've become accustomed to getting your basic sound working, once it's 'second nature', you can start thinking about how fx, modelling, sampling etc could enhance things and introduce it a little at a time until it becomes second nature.

Get to know the Sound Engineer – it's a title that goes with the job of sitting at the mixer desk and making sure things sound generally OK for the punters – the person doing this may or may not be an experienced sound technician but he needs to be your best friend for the night. His task is the sound that goes out to the audience, concentrate on creating your sound onstage and let him worry about what the audience hears. The worst thing band members can do is wander to the back of the hall and listen to the rest of the band – resist the temptation to do this and you'll be much happier.

First, set up the drums, back-line, the monitors and PA, and make sure everything is functioning. Don't immediately think that the drums are over loud and need damping – an empty hall will reflect percussion with a vengeance but even a small crowd will soon soak up that snare and cymbal crash and even in small venues it usually helps to have the kick drum mic'd but sound check your onstage levels without this in the monitors where you'll need it later. Your band should line up with the bass player to the drummer's left as it's the best eye-line for the drummer, who needs eyes-on the bass part of the band's rhythm section. Convention puts the lead guitar to the bass player's left with the rhythm guitar on the drummer's right, (again in line of sight and carefully aimed drumstick!). Vocalist front and centre. There are reasons for this convention - start this way then, if you do move things around, you'll know what's at stake - the rhythm section players need to lock in to the drummer. Once you have developed an instinctive understanding through practice and experience you'll be free to roam. Guitarists remember, too, that your backline amp is your 'monitor' - if you can't hear it clearly you'll get lost.

Start with your monitors up *but the PA right down* and send your sound engineer (or a willing volunteer with good ears) into the auditorium. Run through one of your best songs and check that everyone can hear what they need to hear on stage. Check with the sound engineer for how the instrument balance sounded. You'll need to make some compromises if one or two people are unhappy. If so, try moving them, or adjust the monitor positions, check the angle that speaker cabs are facing in, you may need to move people away from something or you may need to move them closer.

Guitarists, don't forget that you have *a tone control* as too much bass will create a muddiness - leave the bassier bass to the man with four strings. You can control tone at the guitar. Many guitar players simply set the tone knob to 'max' and forget about it and at this setting you will get the widest range of frequencies your guitar will produce, but try being more focused, you're not a one-man-band. Single coil pick-ups can, for example, be very bright, sometimes more than you might like; to add some depth simply roll off some top-end with the tone control.

The guitar also has a volume control and it's often used simply as an on-off switch, all or nothing, but it's a variable control, not a toggle switch. It's meant to be versatile, so use it like this:- With the volume control at max, set the amp to the highest gain/volume settings that you intend to use, now turn down the guitar volume control for a cleaner sound for the quieter stuff you play. When you want oomph, get a smooth change by turning your guitar volume control back up. This is a professional technique much used by famous pro players including Jimi Hendrix. While you are checking those maximum amp settings for gain and volume levels, check them rolled back a couple of degrees, too; you'll often find a punchier and more cutting sound waiting for you. It's all too easy to tip over into a more squashed, thrashy, rock-out sound that is much more exciting on-stage than it is for the audience.

Finally, the PA. Everyone imagines this bit *is* the sound check – with all that "one, two, one two" stuff. It's actually the last part. There will be times when due to sharing a bill or time constraints this is all the time you get but usually you'll have time to sound check properly – use it! Remember that the PA should be set up so that the sound for the house can be adjusted separately from that going to the band's monitors (unless you are running your own PA this shouldn't be a issue). Run through a song, this time setting the initial volume for the vocals. They will sound loud without a crowd to soak them up and the sound will bounce back ('reflect') from the rear walls and floors. Adjust the back-line if necessary. Run through the noisiest songs for both vocals and for guitars, checking what happens when effects kick in or heavy distortion launches. Check the quietest bits too. Check drum mic'ing as drums and vocals can clash in the mix. Make sure that acoustic instruments, keyboards, sequencers etc are all set correctly and balanced. This is a time for gentle tweaking and fine tuning, hopefully you'll have created the right balance in the first stage of the sound check! Play through a couple of numbers and make sure that everyone is as happy as possible. Once the crowd is in you'll need to fine tune some more but with the initial balance right, that's the easy part. Once you've set levels - try to ensure that no-one changes them - other acts, things being moved etc.

This, then, is the Band Sound Check and it's always *a compromise*. If it is a time for all to give their opinions, it's very rarely possible for everyone to get exactly what they want so be professional and agree workable compromises; it's no good if people start turning up, or down, later. Both the guy that wants to rock out at 11 and the shy self-conscious player who backs off, share one thing: they can both ruin the mix, your band's sound.

The Sound Check is the time to agree the on-stage sound and once it's set it doesn't get altered unless problems occur later, such as feedback issues or the crowd absorbing more, or less, of the front of house sound than you'd anticipated. This is being professional. The whole band needs to agree *not to change individual settings* once you've decided on the balance. The sound engineer is the only person who should adjust volumes once the balance is set and needs to remember that the mix he can hear in his headphones will sound very different to someone in the middle of a crowded venue. The engineer, though, should never change that agreed on stage sound balance unless individuals have been cranking things up! Communication between band members, and between band and engineer, is essential. If anyone has a problem, use the time between songs to say so and sort it!

Technical Sound Check Stuff

Generally speaking, channel EQ controls should be kept as close to flat (centre position) as possible, especially on mic channels. In any case, start the soundcheck with all channel EQ controls at centre. Adjustments should be made for specific purposes - remember, this is a PA system, not a home stereo (amoung other things, home stereos don't have to produce 110 to 130dB SPLs with zero feedback).

Reverb or echo should be added principally to vocals and in small amounts. Lead guitar, keyboards and horns can sometimes also use small amounts of either effect, but drums and bass guitar should usually be kept "dry" to allow a firm-sounding foundation for the rhythm section.

Final monitor or aux. send levels should be set according to the artists' needs. To get started however, assume that the vocal channels will need to be loudest through the monitors, acoustic guitar will also require a fairly high monitor send setting, but aside from that, other active channels should have lower monitor settings. Drum mic channel monitor sends may be left off at first, then turned up as required. A secondary monitor system, perhaps for keyboards or drums, or multiple monitor systems could be adjusted similarly at first then re-adjusted according to the various artists' wishes.

If there are effects-to-monitor masters, remember that reverb or echo should be added to the monitors in smaller amounts than to the FOH system to avoid feedback.

you are using a stereo mixer, the channel pan controls should be set at center position. The only time you might set them differently would be if you decided to run a mono PA, i.e. with the main power amplifiers all inter-connected to a summed mono output on the mixer. Then you could use the pans to send all the drum mic channels, for instance, to the left sub-master, and the rest of the band to the right sub-master thus creating two sub-mixes to facilitate level adjustments using a MAIN, SUM or MONO bus and master.

Dealing With Sound Problems

If you have done all the preparatory setup work during a sound check, you should not have to ride the channel levels very much. The only levels you should need to change would be instrument solos, backup vocals and seldom-used channels that are kept shut off until needed. Lead vocals may need slight level adjustments if the vocalist has a habit of fading back. If they persist in doing this, a possible solution may be to

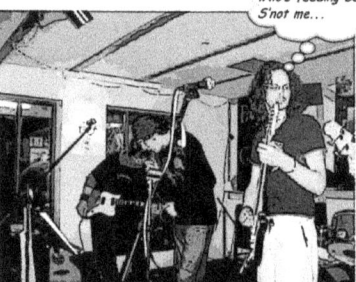
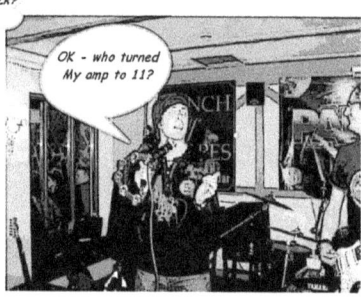

turn that individual down through the monitors, a trick which should cause them to compensate by singing louder and/or getting closer to the mic (just remember to reward them by bringing their monitor level back up). Channel monitor level settings will require some adjustments as well, and roughly the same ones as above. Keep in mind that pre-fader, pre-EQ monitor sends represent an independent mix. So, for example, when the harmonica player is ready to play, you will have to bring that mic channel's level and monitor level up – ditto for horn mic channels, acoustic guitar mic channels, etc. which would normally be left off until needed.

Sound checks are all about getting a band's on-stage sound balance right, but with a crowd in you will need to make some further adjustments as two things will have changed. One, an audience significantly alters the venue's acoustics, and two, the band will be running on adrenalin and likely, despite all the sound-check agreed balances and levels, to be playing louder than usual. It is quite easy, and normal, to play louder without changing any volume settings – drummers don't have volume settings and whilst they are often major culprits here, they can also be reacting to necessary hikes when the band actually needs to be a bit louder.

The audience absorbs a lot of the sound especially the higher frequencies so you will have a different tonal balance than you did with an empty room. Vocals are likely to be getting lost in these new dynamics so the sound engineer should slowly turn them up a little at the mixing desk and adjust tone controls for more clarity. These are technical adjustments, not artistic ones. Slow and gradual adjustments mean the audience won't suffer sudden changes. With a separate monitor mix the band needn't notice any changes either – with vocal levels at least, and, if he's in the house mix, you can turn the bass player up or down for a better overall balance without disturbing the band on-stage.

Although he has *The Final Word*, the sound engineer should make technical adjustments and not artistic decisions but an inexperienced band will often forget the agreed sound check levels and be far too loud in a panicky response to the audience in front of them. If so, the engineer will need to reset their levels.

There are occasions when the band might need to be louder. Again changes need to be gradual - unless there is an obvious glitch such as a gain knob that's been brushed against and has turned itself to 1, or someone who hasn't flicked over a stand-by switch! It happens. Other than problems like that, the engineer must not meddle with the sound on stage as the band have to be able to hear what they are playing; and unless the sound mix is awfully wrong, adjustments should be made between songs so the audience only notices a gradual improvement and not a sudden dramatic change.

The middle of a gig is not a good time to be asking band members to adjust their tone and other settings unless they have reneged on the agreements or there is some unexpected factor that is demanding a change (sometimes using back-up instruments or other technical issues can require this). An interval can be a vital chance to get 'under the bonnet' but don't try to re-engineer the gig completely; focus on simple adjustments to cope with unexpected problems. Issues can arise with power amps, with monitors, gear failure (my band's live 'check list' has over 100 items - plenty of scope for glitches).

Here are ways to approach the most common problems that arise during a gig:

Dealing with Feedback

I'm not referring here to the deliberate generation of individual instrument feedback by a guitarist, but when, at a whole band level, the volume rises, and the sound from the speakers reaches microphones, where it is then amplified and goes round again – is literally *fed back* - and then gets amplified again becoming a painful howl. This is the feedback issue that you need to avoid and **prevention** is far better than having to cure it!

A first line of preventive defence is to use decent vocal mics (such as Shure SM58s)
There is a reason why some microphones are more expensive – and popular. They may be designed and built to be less prone to feedback but their improved build quality and dynamic range, factors which limit the picking up of 'stray' sound, will not prevent feedback if they are incorrectly placed or if other factors leak sound into them.

Have the mics well behind the PA speakers, which must not be pointed at the mics.

Mic handling - Make sure the singer doesn't cover the rear of the microphone mesh with their hand and get them as close to the mic as possible. Watch out for singers who start roaming the whole band area or charging forwards of the speakers. This doesn't mean don't roam, but if its likely then sound check it so that the resulting sound issues are a known quantity.

Mic positioning - Pointing the <u>rear</u> of the vocal mic (on its stand) at the monitors helps as they are designed to be less sensitive in a direct line in this direction hence the 45 degree angle tilt you'll notice vocal mics are usually set at on their stands. This isn't quite the case with hypercardioid microphones - these need to be set at a 45 degree angle to the monitor face so are usually kept level and the monitor itself slightly offset (*see the diagrams*). Your microphone spec sheet will show the best positioning to find it's 'deaf' spot.

Feedback busting -

Assuming everything is done right during the setup and sound check, feedback should not become a problem unless someone gets too close to a speaker with a mic. When that happens, you can probably see which mic it is and know which channel's monitor or PA level to turn down. If it's too close to a monitor, turn down the channel's monitor send level and if it's too close to the FOH speakers pull down the channel's level fader. However, if it's not immediately obvious which mic is responsible, try the following;

If you have set the input channel gains high enough for there to be some clip light activity – see SETUP section 3 item (a) - the light on the channel which is feeding back should be brighter and on more steadily than it was before. Scan the Clip LED's and turn down that channel's monitor send level. If it's a currently unused mic whose channel should be shut off, e.g. a harmonica mic or acoustic guitar mic (did you do an "oops" and leave it on?), any clip light action at all would be an indicator. In this case turn down the monitor sends and pull down the channel fader. But, if you didn't set the gains high enough to use the clip lights, you'll have to make your best guess. Some "usual suspects" include:
• Overhead drum/cymbal mics may be suspect if the drummer has a monitor.
• Try turning down the mic channels' monitor sends. If that works, try using the channel EQ to minimize feedback, but don't deaden the sound too much.
· A singer's acoustic guitar mic might be too close to a monitor.

Since vocal mics tend to pick up some flattop and that gets into the monitors along with the actual guitar mic signal which singers usually want to hear at a goodly level, it's an invitation to feedback. Try turning down the guitar mic channel's monitor send. If your mixer has input phase reversal buttons, try reversing the phase on the guitar mic channel so you can bring the monitor level back up without feedback.

Mixer input phase reversal is sometimes a very effective way to get rid of certain persistent feedback problems. It works when the problem is that two mics are picking up the same source and feeding it into a monitor close to those mics. By putting one (only) of those two channels out of phase, the offending source signal riding on that channel gets cancelled out by the similar signal in the other channel and the problem is solved. If your mixer does not have phase buttons, you can accomplish the same feat by taking one (only) of the offending mic's cable connectors apart and reversing the leads. This is where having your own Sound Engineer comes in handy! Putting a channel or source signal out of phase does not affect the sound.}

If the problem still isn't solved, go to plan B – haul down the monitor master/s. That should solve the problem, but now the band has no monitors. Bring the monitor masters back up to a point below where they were before so they can have some coverage. Of course if lowering the monitor master levels does not work you'll need to lower the main masters. Now it is important to find a quick remedy which will let you get the main or monitor levels back up to where they should be. First, go to your main or monitor EQ. Pull down a few of the sliders slightly (−3dB) in the frequency range which your ears tell you is likely to be the right one. Now ease up the master. If the feedback starts again, lower the master a little, re-centre the EQ faders you just pulled down and try pulling down some other frequencies then bringing the master back up. Eventually, and hopefully soon, you'll have it under control, but now the main or monitor system frequency response has been altered and probably doesn't sound right. Try carefully pushing some of the EQ sliders back up towards centre position – you need to normalize the EQ as much as possible. Do not pull down all the EQ Faders at once – That would be about the same thing as lowering the mixer masters, only much more time consuming and it might even cause new feedback problems later on. If the problem remains that a mic and a speaker have decided to feed back. You still need to find these two culprits then re-position them or insert an EQ in that mic's channel in order to solve the problem properly. This can be done later, but it needs to be done.

There may actually be situations where pulling down the main AND monitor masters fails to end the howling completely. Likely suspects would include feedback from a spare electric guitar and amp or an electric/acoustic guitar and amp waiting to be used and mistakenly left on.

If a guitarist or singer/guitarist insists on leaving their standby electric-acoustic guitar plugged into an amp with it turned on and the volume left up, try (at least) to encourage them to leave their pick in the strings that resonate. It's a simple solution, but it requires knowing which tring(s) to deaden. With flattops, it's most often the low E, A or D string. A better solution, of course, is for them to leave the guitar's volume control turned off or, if it doesn't have one, to turn off the amp's volume control.

Further suspects could be:
• a stuck keyboard note;
• a clavinet or other stringed keyboard instrument and keyboard amp feeding back;
• an unused instrument mic plugged directly into a powered monitor or combo amp, mistakenly left on and feeding back into it.
Any of these problems are impossible to cure from the mixing station. Someone onstage will have to turn down the offending volume control or free-up the stuck key or move the mic – or whatever.

What to do when its all 'A Bit of a Mush...'
There's no real heading for this but you'll soon know when it all sounds a bit squashed and foggy. There are a couple of reasons that are most likely to be at the root of this:-

A high level of sound on stage
When onstage levels are high, the vocal mics will be picking up the instrument amps. If the onstage sound level exceeds 90dB, and it usually will, then some of that sound is going to be louder than the singer. Listen to the PA when the vocalist isn't singing and you can hear the sound that shouldn't be there. This turns your sound to mud and gets worse due to the slight time delay involved. Moving the back-line so it doesn't point directly at any vocal microphones will help - this isn't easy in a small venue but it isn't impossible. As with the feedback issue, good vocal mics also make a world of difference, not picking up that stray sound to the same extent as cheaper, inferior types. It doesn't pay to economise on vocal mics.

Power Amplifiers

The various features of a power amplifier can be broken down into several sections in order to simplify explanations. The sections break down as follows:

General Information

Power Amplifiers have virtually flat frequency response so differences in sound are often more imaginary than real, although some of the ultra-compact amps with "switching" power supplies may not be quite as good at driving subwoofers as the heavier ones with conventional power supplies. Aside from that,however, the only continuing difference between power amplifiers is reliability and even that tends to be less of a variable as designs improve.

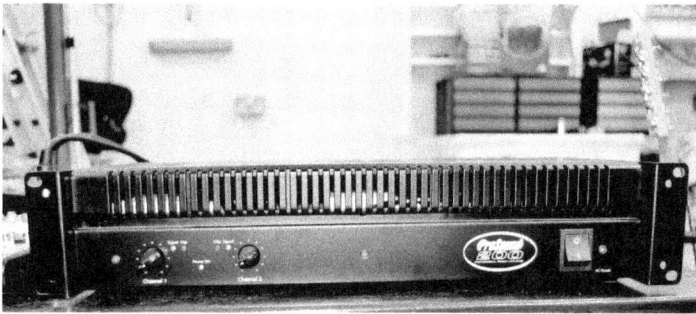

Power Amps: you could need four of these to run a system with an active three way cross-over and monitors. Always carry spare fuses, and ideally gig with a spare amp in reserve!

Mono or Stereo?

Mono power amplifiers are something of a vanishing breed these days, however they do exactly the same job as one channel of a stereo amp in terms of basic sound quality and are still employed in a variety of applications from live PA to installations. They usually have two Speaker Outputs wired in parallel and may have two Inputs also wired in parallel. Dual parallel Inputs are not intended to accept stereo mixer signals. Instead, the extra input can be patched to feed some of the (mono) mixer signal to the input of another power amp - rather like using a "Y" adapter. If you do connect a mixer's stereo outputs to these inputs there can be phase cancellations causing a change in the sound, and possibly distortion. To connect a stereo mixer to a mono power amplifier or one channel of a stereo amp, find a mono output on the mixer and use that. If the mixer does not have a mono output, i.e. One representing the sum of the left and right channels, simply pan all the channels left or right and use the output you've panned to. Also remember that, as with one channel of a stereo amp, connected speakers will be in a parallel circuit even though there are two Output jacks. Hence, if you connect two 8 ohm speakers, the overall speaker impedance will be 4 ohms (more about this later). Stereo power amplifiers can be viewed as two mono amps in the same package. As a result, you can connect two 8-0hm speakers, one to each channel, and the speaker impedance encountered by the amplifier will still be 8 ohms. But connect another 8-ohm speaker to one of the channels and that channel will encounter 4 ohms. And, because each channel can operate quite independently of the other, *channel one* can power a (mono) Front Of House speaker system while *channel two* powers monitors. Stereo FOH PA systems are becoming more common these days, however a mono system works as well in most situations

Power - Which Watts are Which?

Amplifier power ratings these days tend to be in watts expressed as "continuous average" or "burst average" or "peak" or "music power" or "continuous music power", etc. In the old days, the nomenclature was "RMS" which stands for "root mean square" and reflects the results of a test for the amp's long-term, continuous output capability. Other, more modern tests tend to net fairly similar results but are more complex and require more sophisticated equipment. Two ratings which are worth looking for are
Continuous Average Power and Burst Average Power. The first rating will be similar to what an RMS test would net and the second one will be higher, reflecting the amplifier's ability to repeatedly produce clean peaks which last for at least one complete wavelength.

Headroom

A good amp will have 3dB of headroom at its maximum, continuous output. This means that the amp can deliver double that output on frequent, full-wave peaks. That's what really helps to make those deep "thuds" and "rumbles" shake the floor when you are powering subwoofers.

Slew Rate

Slew rate is basically a measure of the amplifier's ability to supply voltage in response to fast, short duration peaks and is measured in volts per microsecond (one millionth of a second). A slew rate of "30VUsec" - 30 Volts per microsecond - is considered good, but anything down to 20 VUsec is also considered good. High frequency reproduction is thought to be better in amplifiers with a high slew rate hence, if you do hear a difference between two amps with radically different slew rates it would be in the highs. However the truth is that slew rates have to be unusually low - well below 10VUsec before any highs are likely to be muted.

Damping Factor

Damping factor is usually, but not very accurately, linked to low frequency reproduction. The popular thinking goes as follows; although an amplifier may have flat frequency response all the way down to 20Hz, its ability to make speakers reproduce low frequencies with maximum sound pressure depends to a certain degree on its damping factor. This is supposedly because amplifier outputs encounter a certain amount of "Counter-EMF" (electro-magnetic force) from the speakers, especially woofers. These induced signal voltages tend to be out of phase with the amplifier's output and can cancel some of it, especially on low-frequency peaks where the cone is travelling very far in and out causing the voice coil to cut more lines of magnetic force hence generating more counter-EMF voltage. Damping factor, in its popular perception, reflects an amplifier's potential ability to counter or "damp" the effects of this process thus permitting more power to be delivered to the woofers. There is some truth to this, but not as much as you might think. Damping factor is a matter of impedances. As long as the amplifier's output impedance is lower than the overall speaker impedance you have damping. The method of calculating an amplifier's damping factor is based on the difference between the two impedances. If, for example, an amplifier's output impedance is 0.01 Ohms and it is designed to operate into a 4-Ohm impedance, the damping factor would be 4 / 0.01= 400. A high damping factor, though, does not guarantee better bass response from the speakers. That characteristic can be chalked up to large amounts of power "headroom". In fact a really high damping factor can have an effect on the woofers which makes their lowest frequencies roll off more abruptly than if they were being powered by an amp with low damping, the net result being a reduction in deep bass response. Once again, check the specs for headroom figures. **A good amp will have 3dB of headroom at its maximum, continuous output.** This means that the amp can deliver double that output on frequent, full-wave peaks.

Power At Impedence

An amplifier varies its maximum output capability in accordance with the overall speaker impedance it is driving. Solid state amplifiers do this inversely to changes in the speaker impedance (yes, speaker impedances actually change with the frequencies they are reproducing - more about that in the Speaker section). In other words, as the impedance decreases, a solid-state amp is able to put out more power, and as it increases the opposite happens. Tube amps have a "favoured" impedance above or below which their maximum power capability decreases. It would seem to follow that solid state amplifiers might be able to deliver more than their rated power if you connected them to very low impedances. But we all know that this is not the case - especially if we've had an amp shut down or, Heaven forbid, blow up because the speaker load was too low. What happens is, the amp actually tries to put out more power than it was designed to deliver. It overheats in the process and will self-destruct if it has no thermal protection circuitry to shut it down or otherwise limit its activity. Conversely, amps are not harmed when connected to high load impedances; their maximum output is simply reduced. And when a solid-state amplifier is connected to no speakers at all, in other words an infinitely high impedance, it won't put out any power at all, it just takes a holiday. Tube amps are very different in this regard. They will self-destruct if run with no load connected.

Be sure that the overall speaker impedance being driven by each amplifier channel is not lower than the manufacturer's specification. If the rating is much too low for your amp to handle it may cause serious problems for your power amplifiers. On the other hand, if it is only a little lower than the amp's minimum rating, you might be alright..

A Common Question...

"If I connect too many speakers, will it ruin my amp?"

Oddly enough the answer is, not necessarily. You could, for example, run as many as four 8-ohm speakers from one channel of an amplifier, assuming it has a minimum load rating of 2 ohms per channel. And by making a special series/parallel wiring rig, you could theoretically run as many speakers as you like from one amplifier, however it could be a wiring nightmare. Before we leave this subject it's worth mentioning that a rough rule-of-thumb regarding power at impedance goes as follows: double the speaker impedance and you cut the amp's output in half - cut the impedance in half and (assuming it's not too low now) you double the amp's output. Again, this is a very rough rule because all amplifiers react differently to speaker impedance changes and almost none of them puts out exactly half or double power into double or half the impedance. If you are in doubt about what an amplifier delivers into a certain impedance, check the manufacturer's specifications.

Passive & Active Cooling

In the beginning, all power amplifiers were passively cooled. With passive cooling, the output transistors are tightly fastened to metal fin clusters called heat-sinks attached to the outside of the amp. As air passes over the fins, heat from the output transistors is radiated away. If there is restricted air flow, the result can be overheating and possibly damage. Passive cooling is common on units rated at under 800 watts; however, in power amplifiers over 800 watts, active cooling is the norm. *Although proper ventilation is important to all amplifiers, it is critical to those which are passively cooled. Racks or cases should always be open-backed and placed well away from walls or other obstructions.*

In an actively cooled amp, a built-in fan moves the air across compact, internal heat-sinks. The chassis (case) of the amp helps to trap the air inside and further ensure that it travels over the fins. In most of the newer amplifiers, fans tend to be thermally regulated so that they either rotate slowly or nor at all when the amp is running cool. This way, the long-term amount of dust drawn in by the fan is reduced. Dust sticking to internal heat-sinks can act as an insulator and reduce their thermal transfer. It may be worthwhile to have a technician clean the internal heat-sinks once every two years or so if your amplifier does not have an air filter. *Clean or replace the air filter regularly. This will prevent it from getting clogged with dust, choking off cool air.*

Power Amplifiers Features & Specifications

Inputs

Most PA power amplifiers today offer a selection of input connectors and facilities. Balanced inputs may take the form of 3-pin XLR's and/or 1/4 inch TRS (tip-ring-sleeve - a.k.a. "stereo") jacks. As a rule there will be both and the 1/4 inch jack will be wired parallel with the XLR so that you can patch to the input of another mixer or to the other channel's input on the same stereo power amp (a Stereo/Mono button can make this unnecessary - see below). Some amplifiers such as the old Beta-800 have an input feature which utilizes internal wiring and a special switching jack, usually the B channel input, to patch the two channels together. The amp operates with both channels reproducing the same (mono) *signal until a jack is inserted in the B input which* breaks the internal patch so that the channels will be independent.

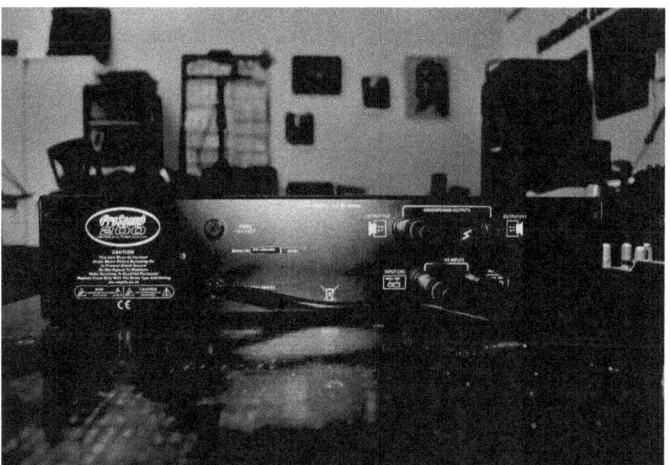

The emphasis on designing features into stereo amplifiers which make them easy to convert to what might be called "dual-channel mono" operation further illustrates that this does tend to be the way they are often employed outside the living room. "Bridging" (not to be confused with dual-channel mono operation) is another way of turning a stereo amp into a mono amp, in this case with the power of both channels combined into one output signal. Although modern PA amplifiers tend to have a Bridge switch, some may not in which case it is necessary to connect a mono mixer signal to both channels either using a "Y" adapter or by patching to the other channel via the additional input if there is one. Then you reverse the phase of the signal going into the other channel. This is accomplished by taking the cable-end apart and resoldering the leads in reverse order. If you're using balanced patch cables, reverse the "phase" and "reverse phase" wires. In an unbalanced line, reverse the hot and ground wires.

Be very careful about bridging - it can be difficult even for people who are familiar with it. Read the "Bridging" section below.

Outputs

Output connections on PA amplifiers include 1/4-inch jacks to post (a.k.a. "banana") terminals, to 3-pin XLR connectors, to combination XLR/1/4-inch connectors, to the "Speakon" locking connectors developed by Neutrik in Switzerland. Post terminals carry plenty of power and have been the standard speaker output connection for many years, however there are two problems with them. First, cables have to be either bare-ended and wrapped around the terminals, or equipped with "banana" connectors. In either case the other end of the cable will need to have whatever connector matches the ones on the speakers, though often speakers today can accommodate a variety of these options. Be aware -you *can* receive a very nasty shock by touching post terminals while a kilowatt-plus amp is in use and for this reason expect to see binding posts disappear from power amps. This leaves XLRs and Speakons. XLRs work fine, but due to the cables' resemblance to

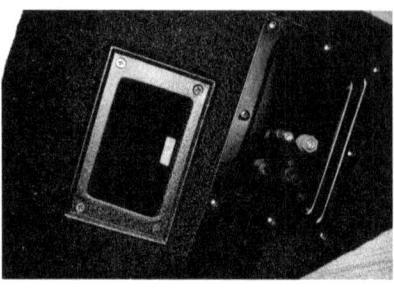
Speaker cab with choice of Speakon, 1/4" jack or post to post cabling.

mic cables, people occasionally use the wrong ones to connect speakers - <u>mic cables</u> just heat up and waste power, assuming they don't melt. Speakon connectors are specifically engineered as speaker cabling and are the likeliest candidate for eventual standardisation - certainly the best - and the most expensive - solution but not all amps/speakers are built to use them.

Level Controls

The function of power amp Level controls is simple enough, the only question is how and why they should be used. For most PA applications you would run them at maximum, reason being that you want the amplifier's full output capabilities available. Or separate channels could be set differently as when driving a monitor mix when the amp channel driving the drummer's monitors could be at max and the other channel at a lower setting for the other monitors.

Mono Stereo Switch

In the "mono" position, this feature ties the two channels' inputs together via internal wiring so that they operate in unison, a.k.a. mono. Mono is a common amplifier operating mode for PA applications involving multiple speakers. If, for instance, you needed to power four subwoofers and four full-range enclosures, you would employ two amplifiers in mono mode, one fed by the low frequency output from the electronic crossover and the other from the crossover's high-frequency output. You would then connect half of the subwoofers to one channel of their power amp, and the other half to the other channel.

The full range speakers would be similarly connected to their amplifier. In the "stereo" position, the switch bypasses the internal input patching so that the channels function independently.

Bridge Switch & Bridging

This feature does almost exactly the same thing as the Mono/Stereo switch but with a major difference (in fact, it is often combined into a mono/stereo/bridge switch); its input-to-input internal patch wiring has the positive and negative leads reversed so that one of the channels is 180 degrees out of phase with the other. *If your system is sounding mysteriously "weak", especially in bass response, check the Bridge switch. If it's "on" and you haven't performed all the following procedures, switch it "off". That weird, weak sound would be caused by acoustic phase cancellations between your speakers.*

Bridging is the process of turning a *two-channel* amplifier into a *one-channel* amplifier producing the summed output of both channels. This is accomplished as follows:-

> Feed the same (i.e. mono) mixer signal to both inputs, but reverse the phase of the signal going into one of the channels. This is not necessary if you have a Bridge switch; it takes care of phase reversal automatically. But if you don't have a Bridge switch, you'll need to do this by taking the plug apart going into the "other" channel's input (i.e.

not the channel directly receiving the mixer signal), unsoldering the wires, reversing the plug leads, resoldering and then plugging it in.

> Check the impedance of the speaker (yes, only one speaker, read on) and divide it by two. This is very important because a bridged amplifier reacts to the connected load at half its value. A 4-ohm load, for example, will seem like 2 ohms to a bridged amplifier and it will react accordingly.

> Check the resulting impedance against the amplifier's minimum load rating. Never connect a load which is lower than that rating.

> If the amp can handle that load, connect the speaker as follows: take the "hot" (+) signal only from each channel and connect your speaker so that the cable end from one channel goes to the "+" speaker terminal and the other cable end goes to the other speaker terminal. Note which channel is driving the "+" speaker terminal so that you will be able to rig another bridged amp and speaker the same way and they will be in phase (VERY important, especially for subwoofers). If your amp has post terminal outputs this is easy; simply connect the two RED terminals, no black ones. If it has 1/4-inch jack socket outputs, you will need to rig a split speaker cable with two 1/4- inch plugs at one end, each plug connected only by the tip tab (the shorter of the two tabs inside the plug). Each plug would then be inserted in a single output jack socket from each channel. If the amp has XLR outputs, rig a split cable as above but with two XLR ends. Check the manufacturer's output code in the amp manual to find out which XLR pin is "+" and solder the cable ends to those terminals in the connectors, once again, only one connector per cable end. Then plug a cable-end XLR into each channel's output XLR and connect the speaker at the other end of the cable. If the amplifier has Speakon outputs and it doesn't have a separate "Bridged" output, follow the same basic procedure as with XLR connectors (except, of course, using Speakons). In any case, attach whichever connector is needed to the speaker end of the split cable. Again, be sure to note
which channel is driving the "+" speaker terminal if you will be bridging another amp and speaker, so that they will be in phase.

> Set both level controls at **MAXIMUM**.

> IMPORTANT!

DO NOT ENGAGE THE BRIDGE SWITCH UNLESS YOU HAVE PERFORMED THE ABOVE FUNCTIONS. Once again, the Bridge switch only patches the two channels' Inputs together and puts one of them out of phase. It does NOT somehow "double your power". In fact, with the two channels out of phase and just running speakers in the normal manner, you would be WASTING power because the speakers connected to them will ALSO be out of phase and CANCEL EACH OTHER OUT acoustically. This can cause up to a 3dB loss in sound pressure which is equivalent to LOSING HALF THE POWER from that amplifier.

> And if, after all this, you still think that bridging two 1,000-watt amps is preferable to using one 2,000-watt amp unbridged, you might consider seeking psychiatric help. The practice of bridging harks back to a time when the most powerful stereo amps only put out around 700 watts in total and had to be bridged in order to get all of it into a speaker. This is no longer a problem.

Limiter Switch

Distortion is damaging to woofers, horn drivers and tweeters, even at applied power levels well below their power ratings. A distorted amplifier signal causes the voice coil to move back and forth erratically in the magnet gap, sometimes contacting the wall of the gap and becoming damaged. This isn't 'going up to 11' - squared or clipped wave forms contain higher levels of current in the delivered power which effectively raises the heating effect, burning the voice coils. Although some speaker systems have fuses and/or circuit breakers to help the drivers survive distortion, the result is the same - an interrupted gig. Compressor/limiters can be set so that the amplifiers never receive enough mixer signal to drive them into damaging distortion levels. *If you have an amplifier or amplifiers with this feature, switch it on and leave it on. A good, sonically transparent, built-in limiter will save you untold speaker failures and cost you absolutely no performance. In fact, limiters can actually maximize clean power.*

Ground Strap

Ground loops and their attendant hum can sometimes be traced to a rack of power amplifiers. If this is the case, try lifting the ground straps on all but one of the amps in the rack. If that fails to cure or sufficiently reduce the noise, re-connect all the Ground Straps and check elsewhere. Do not leave the ground straps off unless you have to.

"Clip" LED

Most manufacturers set the threshold of their Clip LED's to fire at 3 decibels (dB) below the point of distortion. As a result, small amounts of Clip light activity are likely to be acceptable, however check your manual to be sure. In amplifiers with built-in limiters, Clip LED activity can indicate that the limiter is working.

"Protect", "Temp." or "Fault" LEDs

In most cases these lights indicate problems at the outputs created by low or shorted speaker loads. But they are often triggered by output transistor heat levels and can therefore indicate other conditions such as inadequate cooling due to poor ventilation, dirty heatsink fins, a non-functioning fan or a clogged fan filter (clean or change these regularly). If these lights flash briefly on power up, it may not indicate a problem.Some amplifiers are designed to go through a status check when turned on - read your manual to be sure. If these lights come on while the amp is running, you may have a serious problem. Try the following:

1 Disconnect the speaker cables and see if the light goes out. If it does, the problem could be in the speaker circuit - possibly a short circuit somewhere. Use your volt-ohm meter or multimeter to check the overall load resistance. If it is very low or the numbers on a digital meter seem confused, it probably is a short. Now check everything including the cables and connectors as well as the cabinets themselves.
2 If disconnecting the speaker lines does not make the trouble light go out, check the ventilation. If the amp is in a rack or a case, make sure the back is open and away from the wall or any other obstruction. If the amp is fan-cooled, make sure the fan is turning and the filter is clean. If the problem persists, get the amp to a repair shop.

Circuit Breakers and Fuses

By the time a breaker or fuse blows, it's likely that something bad has already happened, unless it's a speaker output fuse (some older amps have them) in which case try turning down the volume. But if it's the AC power fuse or breaker, replacing the fuse or resetting the breaker probably won't help, at least not for long. It is most likely time for a visit to the shop, especially if the problem persists. Although most PA amplifiers have some form of speaker protection built in, you may inadvertently defeat it by repeatedly trying to reset the power breaker or, Heaven forbid, trying to hold it in with something, or wrapping the blown fuse in foil (argh!). One thing which is sure to pop the mains fuse or breaker is blown output transistors and when they short out in the process of blowing they can let all the DC voltage which is stored in the amplifier's filter capacitors go straight out to the speakers. This is called "DC offset" and it instantly turns delicate voice coil wire into a black, motionless, silent mass. Even speakers with fuses or breakers built in may succumb to DC from a big amplifier, so treat popped AC breakers and fuses with respect.

The issue of tone

The aim of good sound engineering is to separate the band's instruments in tone. Guitars with too much middle will fight with the vocals; and, if guitarists have their bass setting high, especially with an open backed cab, and the bass player has his lower mid range well up, this heavy energy will dominate the stage especially if there is keyboards with lots of full left hand chords! This could be an artistic decision if you want to be exceptionally heavy, but experiment with all the options available to you and try for an optimised setting with light as well as shade if you want a cleaner sound. A fully mixed system gives you the option of separating all the instruments in space by using the pan controls. Ideally, this is one for the engineer to rehearse with the band or sound checks could take hours.

With two principal guitarists swapping roles you'll sometimes get the issue of one or both complaining that they can't hear themselves clearly, or that the audience can't hear them distinctly from each other. We've looked already at the on-stage sound factors and remedies but if both have simply set tone controls to the max and use similar amp settings and fx, try a little variety and personalisation. Colour them differently, sonically speaking! Especially effective for the front of house sound is separating them in the mix using the pan controls - as mentioned above.

Using A Crossover

Crossovers are used to send only the relevent part of the 'sound spectrum' to the appropriate PA speaker. The 'sound spectrum' can be divided into two or more frequency bands, Usually three bands – the 'top', 'mids' and 'bottom end' – are separated for a speaker stack, top going to the 'tweeters' – the horns, mids to the mid range cabs and bottom end to the 'woofers' – the bass drivers. Crossovers prevent bass frequencies from damaging (through overloading) the more sensitive mid and top end drivers and help to create a more defined and controllable sound 'picture', ensuring that the higher frequencies are not lost amongst the lower ones. The simplest type of crossover is passive circuitry built into speaker cabs, the frequency bands being separated by way of electronic filters. This is generally a feature of smaller, lower powered systems. 'Active' crossovers, requiring their own power suppy, are used for bigger PA systems, these also require their own power amps – one each for the low, mid and top end of the audio frequency range.

Crossovers are connected between the mixer and power amplifiers. The term "between" means mixer output to unit's input and unit's output to power amp's input(s). There are simple processors which provide pre-equalization for specific speaker systems. They are connected between the mixer and power amp(s) in the same manner as an equalizer. Adjustable *active* crossovers are connected the same way but their outputs must go to separate power amps or amp channels each driving the appropriate woofers, horns and tweeters, or subwoofers and full-range enclosures.

Getting Technical...

Chances are there'll be one guy in your band who is never happier than when he's got a soldering iron in one hand and a screwdriver in the other, surrounded by bits and pieces that used to be a speaker, or amplifier... this bit is for him. If you don't have one, there's stuff here that you'll really need to know – or at least be aware of – before you start cabling together expensive PA components. We have our own (Un)Sound Engineer who can fix, rewire, change fuses and, most importantly, prevent us from making mistakes that can cost thousands. He runs on Guiness and isn't infallible – we once had our stage monitors catch fire mid-gig – but he's saved us from more potential disasters than we can collectively remember. Find yourself one of these, treasure him – or her – give them a title like Chief Roadie, Road Manager or whatever and have them recce for you. Your gigging life will become easier: one thing that can absolutely be guaranteed is that equipment will break down, cut-out, feed back for no readily apparent reason or simply show no inclination to power-up or produce sound at all – all this on a regular basis. Be prepared.

Matching Speakers to Amplifiers...

Will it improve the sound and will it destroy my amplifier? How can you get to be really loud? Read on...

First, The Ohm Thing

Ohms are about resistance. How easily will electricity flow through something and how much current will it draw. Everything electrical has a resistance, light bulbs have ohms, electric ovens have ohms and even drummers have ohms. Lots of ohms means that electricity has trouble getting through and less ohms mean that electricity storms through. Sweaty drummers have fewer ohms and are easier to electrocute. Single loudspeakers usually have eight ohms, though you can buy them with four or with sixteen. (Just in case of confusion I ought to explain about impedance. Speakers are often described as having an impedance of eight ohms, this is because some of their ohms come from speakers being electromagnets. This is more complicated than you need in a musicians guide so for us ohms , resistance and impedance are the same thing.)

Now - How Many Speakers Can I Safely Connect?

If you connect two speakers in parallel (more on this later) then there are two routes that the electricity from the amplifier can go through and there will be twice as much power - right? Three speakers and three times as much, four speakers, five... Actually this is pretty much what *can* happen but before you get carried away you should think about the poor amplifier. A 100W amplifier is still only a 100W amplifier. If it is a solid state (transistor) amp it will bravely try to go on pushing more and more power through your speakers. Transistor amps will try to deliver **double the power every time you halve the ohms**. Eventually they will run out of steam. What happens next depends upon the detailed design. Most will have protection and will just limit their own power/distort or blow a fuse. (**never go to a gig without spare fuses**) With many of them the power supply will be inadequate for the power demand so they only develop their max power into a speaker with the right number of ohms. This means you are wasting your time trying to squeeze more power out. The worst case if you try to add too many speakers is that the output transistors will overheat and fry. FETs are less likely than silicon transistors to do this, but if you understood that sentence you don't need me to explain.

If you have a **valve amp** then the situation is that you must match the output to the speaker and fortunately you have a transformer inside the amp to do this. The deadly thing for valve amps is too high an impedance, too many ohms. Well designed valve amps should have multiple tappings on the output transformer and you really should try to match the ohms on the amp and the speakers. As a general rule most amplifiers will deal with four ohms with no bother although depending on the power supply they may be happier with eight. If you have two speaker cabinets of eight ohms then wiring them up in parallel will give you four ohms and your amp should deal with this happily. The problem would come if you tried to plug in three cabs. Now you have three speakers with only two and a bit ohms, you could be demanding three times the power from your poor amp. Don't do this unless you have calculated the overall impedance and are happy that your amp can cope. If in doubt contact the manufacturer and find out if the amp will cope with low impedances (anything less than four ohms).

If you have a **combo amp** with a built in speaker and an outlet socket for an extension speaker things can get a little more complex. On some combos the socket has a switch so that the internal speaker is disconnected (my Peavey does this). This means I can ignore the ohms of that speaker and just use the Peavey as if it were a head. If your combo leaves the speaker connected when you plug in a lead (which you can tell as the sound will still come out of that speaker) then any speaker will be in parallel with the internal speaker and you need to work out the ohms of the two speakers combined to make sure it doesn't go too low. Fortunately manufacturers don't usually provide a socket for an extension speaker if the amp won't take it so you can be pretty confident about plugging in your extra speaker. Just like with a head amp don't just plug in in two extra speakers as with the internal speaker this makes three and you could damage some amps.

Having too many speakers will only damage amps at high volumes. In any practical situation the damage is almost always caused by too much power. Turn the volume right down at first until you know everything is working and turn the volume up a little at a time listening for any distortion you are not expecting.

There are ways of connecting more than two cabs to an amp by using series connection though you will need special leads to do this. Before you try this you should read the section on series and parallel. In any case you should ask yourself why you want to do this for an instrument amp.

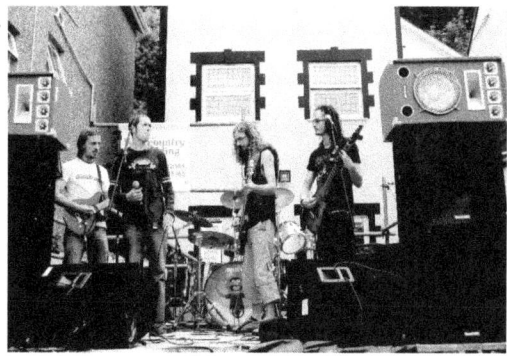

Homs, mids, subs & monitors.

Will This Be Louder?

Yes probably. But it is not completely straightforward. Loudness is subjective because we are more sensitive to some frequencies of sound than others. New speakers may give a smoother sound and seem quieter. Secondly speakers vary quite a lot in their efficiency, that is in how well they turn the electricity from your amp into sound. In practice it is quite possible for the most efficient speakers to make 10 watts sound like 100 watts do from less efficient speakers.

How Loud Can I Go?

If you play gigs then you only need to match the volume of the other instruments if your band is to sound balanced. The best band in the world will sound rubbish if they are not properly mixed. In practice **the critical point for most bands comes when your sound matches the drummer**. Any louder and the drums will need to be miked through the PA to match you. If your PA can deal with this then you are in a whole new ball game. You might as well get the extra sound for all of the instruments through the PA which will give you the chance of having someone mix you properly and achieving a balanced sound. **Keeping the onstage sound down to manageable levels and letting the PA do the work makes sense at every level.**

Even fairly modest combos will produce over 100dB of sound which is more than enough to damage your hearing. Do you really need to be louder? Is hearing important to musicians? I think you know that one. Adding extra speakers should be about the quality of sound for most of us not just a mad pursuit of power.

How Safe Are The Speakers?

So far this has all been about protecting the amp from too few ohms (too many speakers). Now I want to look at matching the speakers to the amp. There are many ways to damage a speaker but the amp only has two ways. It can cook the speaker by passing too much power for too long or it can pop the speaker by pushing it right out of its frame. Most instrument speakers and professional PA speakers are designed so that they can not be pushed out of their frames but hi-fi speakers often aren't. Don't play guitar through your hi-fi unless you want an excuse to buy new speakers. Very low notes do demand that the speaker cones have to move further though, so using bass or keyboards with guitar speakers at high volumes can also cause problems.

Burning out your speakers is much more likely. You have to match the power output of your amplifier to the maximum power handled by the speakers. Power is measured in watts and you need to make sure that you are dealing with real watts. Real watts are RMS watts, ignore anything which says music power, peak watts, PMPO or anything other than RMS. RMS measures the maximum output your amp will produce without distortion. Being a guitarist of course means you will want distortion or overdrive. This effectively adds to the power your amp is generating in fact with distortion your amp will generate up to 1.414 times the RMS output. If you want your speakers safe then it means you need at least one and a half times the power handling in your speakers. This means that a thirty watt amp should have speakers that can handle at least 45 Watts and a 100w amp should be matched with at least 150W speakers. In practice I always try to go for double the power handling, ie 200W speakers with a 100W amp. It is absolutely safe to use big speakers with a small amp though: 200W speakers are fine with a 10W practice amp.

Series And Parallel

Ok this is the ever so slightly (more) technical bit. Speakers have a positive and a negative terminal. This is so that we know which way they go when we apply an electrical current to them from the amplifier. If we connect the positives together and the negatives together then they are con-nected *in parallel*. This would generally be the case for monitor and PA speakers - the first receives the signal from the power amp, the second is linked to the first, the third to the second and so on. The positives are always connected to the tips of jack plugs and are usually marked with a + or a red dot on the speaker itself. Speakers though may be connected by 'speakon' cabling, by jack ended speaker cable or by speaker wire, the wires bound onto posts.

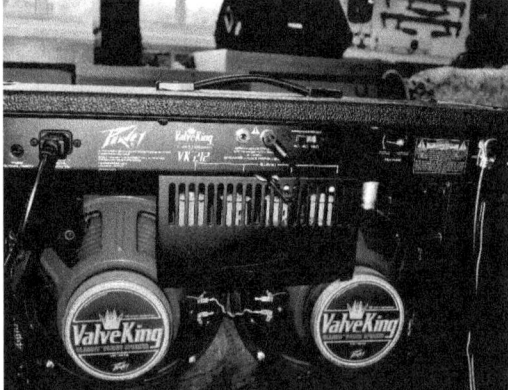

Rear of my 212 guitar combo - note the series connection wiring between the speakers.

Parallel Connection

Connecting speakers in this way has a number of effects:

\# You increase the volume of sound.
\# The impedance is reduced below that of the lowest speaker.
\# The amplifier will have to supply more current.
\# The power handling (the watts) are doubled

To calculate the new impedance you need to use a bit of algebra and know the impedance of all the speakers, R1 ,R2, R3 etc. to calculate the new overall or total impedance Rtot the formula is

$$\frac{1}{Rtot} = \frac{1}{R1} + \frac{1}{R2} + \frac{1}{R3}$$

If you had two speakers and they are both 8ohms the calculation is:

$$\frac{1}{Rtot} = \frac{1}{8} + \frac{1}{8} = \frac{1}{4}$$

So Rtot =4ohms

Fortunately we usually only connect up speakers with the same ohms in parallel so that if you divide the ohms of a single speaker by the number of speakers in parallel then this gives you the overall impedance. So three 8ohm speakers in parallel would be 8/3 or 2.6667 ohms. Anything more complicated and you have to do the sums.

Series connection

The positive on one speaker is connected to the negative on the next one. They make a daisy chain. The plug is connected to the positive on one speaker and the negative of the other, pin to positive still.

Series connection also makes changes:

The ohms increase
The sound level decreases
The current from the amp decreases
The power handling is doubled.

Calculating the ohms is easy, just add them together. For example two 4ohm speakers give you 8ohms.

The final method of connecting speakers that you will come across with musical instruments is used as a useful way of connecting four speakers without reducing the ohms too much. Effectively you are just combining the two ways we have already looked at and it is called series/parallel. This is the classic 4x12 connection. First connect pairs of speakers in parallel. Then connect the two pairs of speakers in series as if they were single speakers.

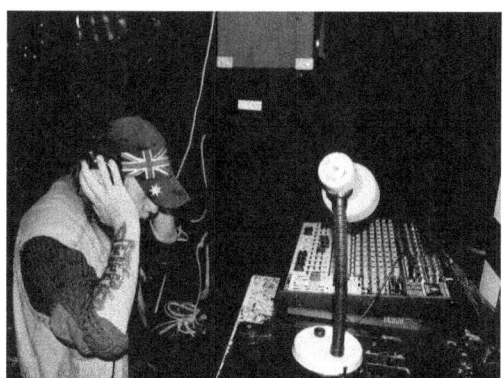

     If you have a couple of 2x12 cabs and you want to connect them together then this would be a good way to go about it. If the internal wiring is in series then no problem, if they are internally wired in parallel, and they probably are, then you need your repair shop to make a lead up to connect them in series.

If you want to calculate the impedance you need to do it in two parts, first caculate the impedance of each parallel pair then add them together. In practice if all the speakers are the same then the ohms will be the same as for a single speaker.

This is a really useful way of doing things because you get double the sound of a single speaker without using any extra power from the amplifier or having to drive a really low impedance speaker. The power handling is four times that of a single unit. The disadvantage? You have to pay for and carry four speakers at a time.

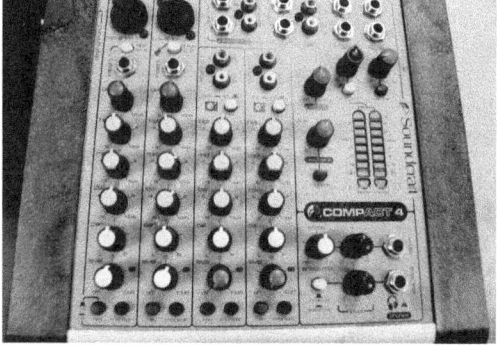

Sound Mixing

Just as it helps to have a techie on board it also helps to have your own sound man/woman/girl (our (un)sound engineer fills both roles (albeit carrying a card to prove he's human) and chances are this may well be the same person for you too. Look for the guy that doesn't get out much, this could be his finest hour. Sound engineering is beyond the scope nof this book, and if you're just starting out as a band it's going to be way beyond what you need to be getting involved with. There are many excellent books for anyone who really wants to be the guy sat the desk with the headphones on. Right now you need to understand what does what and, very broadly, why...

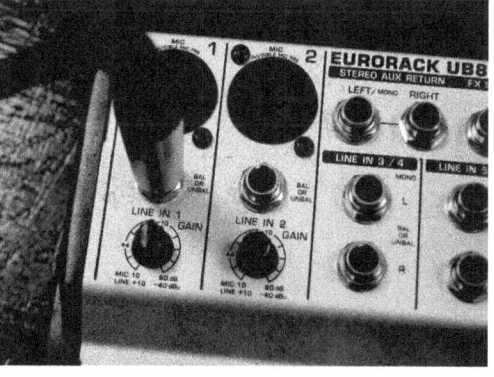

The PA Mixer
At the most simple level, a PA system comprises speaker cabinets, a power amplifier and some means of mixing microphone and instrument signals to feed the amplifier. There will be some form of volume level control for each input, some form of tone control and the ability to connect with external kit such as equalizers,

effect processors, limiters and also a stage monitoring system. A simple powered mixer will provide several channels with inputs for both XLR and ¼" jack for each one (you need to choose one or the other for a channel input, you can't plug into both!). There will be a level control for the output from each channel and also, often, a control for the amount of any effects to be applied to the channel. Where effects are included, usually reverb and chorus, there will be a selection switch for the type – this is generally one choice that covers any channel for which effects have been selected. Another 'universal' control is the master level for the output of all channels 'in the mix' and, where there is an output for monitoring, a control for the level applied to this also. For a low powered PA, mixers like this can handle several microphones along with acoustic guitars and keyboards, and are a feature of many commercial rehearsal rooms. Solo artists and small combos can happily gig with such a set-up and it is also a convenient way for a band to run it's on-stage monitoring. To put more in the mix though you will need 'a desk'.

The Mixing Desk De-Mystified

What does a Mixer actually do?

A mixer, mixing console, mixing board or desk is a device that allows you to balance, position, effect and equalize various different audio channels into one sonic image - a mix. You can add FX to selected channels, position instruments to a location in the stereo field (pan), route channels to external FX units and shape the sound of each channel with a dedicated equalizer allowing you to adjust the bass, treble and mid range.

The first piece of 'band' kit we bought, as opposed to individual pieces of kit, was a mixer. Lots of venues have their own, as an integral part of the PA system, but many don't, or - if they do, they often turn out to be less than perfect - with channels that don't work, sticky faders, dodgy connections. The first gig we played, we found on setting up that the house mixer didn't work at all ie - no PA. We simply plugged in our trusty beast and left it to our own (un)sound engineer to sort out. At other gigs it's proven a better desk than the resident one or it's mixed our stage sound for us. Inexpensive digital mixers, like ours, include mic preamps, phantom power and the ability to record from the desk. We can also use it to get tracks onto a home pc for DIY recording projects and a wide variety of loops, samples and FX that we can trigger live. Get one. Now.

Now, this will make a whole lot more sense if you are *looking at a mixer* – and hopefully far more sense than the manual does (been there, bought the t-shirt etc)...

Mixer Terminology

First, the INPUTS:

"MIC"

The microphone input is usually low-impedance, i.e. 5000 ohms or less in mixers with active input circuitry or approximately 600 ohms in mixers with input transformers (Note: there is no problem with plugging a 600 ohm or lower impedance microphone into a 5,000 ohm input). It will usually have a 3-pin "XLR" connector and it will always be a female XLR (male XLR's are always outputs). Mic inputs may also be 1/4-inch "phone" jacks in older or smaller mixers, however they may be high-impedance (over 5000 ohms) so check the owner's manual. A high impedance ("HI Z") mic may produce a low level or distorted sound when connected to a low impedance ("LOW Z") input. A low Z mic in a high Z input can produce similar results. If you have a low Z mic and only high Z inputs are available, a "low-to-high Z" adapter can be used to overcome the problem. The channel input gain control or input attenuator on mixers with such features, will always regulate the "mic" input. And you may find a phantom switch near the Mic input or somewhere in the master section. This feature applies a small amount of DC voltage to one of the Mic input connector leads – usually 24 – 48 Volts. This travels backwards up the cable to the mic (the only time electrons flow "upstream") for the purpose of powering a condenser mic.

"LINE"

Line inputs are always high-impedance (10,000 ohms or more) and employ 1/4″ jacks or sometimes RCA (phono) jacks. This is where you would connect a high-impedance mic or the line-level output of a signal source. The term "line-level" is used to cover signals referenced to 0dBm or 0.773 Volts rms. These are much greater than those produced by mics or instrument pickups which produce signals down around 0.1 Vrms or less. The range of things which produce line-level output signals is very wide. Almost, anything which runs on AC or DC power produces this level of signal. The exception would be the output of a "phantom" power supply which is mic-level. Beware of "speaker" outputs or "extension" speaker outputs as even the smallest amplifier produces too much power for a "line" input and will overload the circuitry. Also, remember to use shielded cables with a centre lead wrapped in the shield wire (as opposed to speaker cables which only have two regular leads). They help minimize hum and noise when connecting line outputs to line inputs. The channel input gain control or input attenuator on most mixers will regulate the "line" inputs and the input circuits have sufficient gain for high-impedance microphones. You may need to set the Input Gain control higher for high Z mics than line-

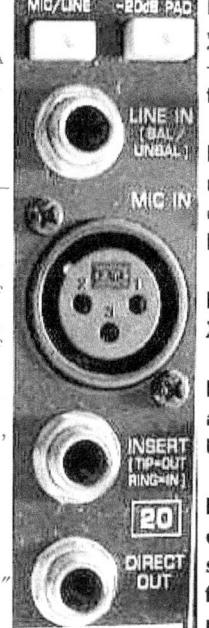

Mic/Line: switch it to the source you are using

-20 Pad: If the signal is too hot for the preamp, kick it in

Line In: For synths, drum machines, external preamps, and other devices that output line level.

Mic In: For your mic. This is an XLR jack

Insert: This is both an input and an output. Takes a TRS cable. Unbalanced (always)

Direct Out: This is a line level output. Typically it is balanced, so it also takes a TRS cable. Good for connecting to multi-track recorders, even soundcards

level sources but some mixers have Mic/Line selector switches so that the Gain settings can be roughly the same for mics and line-level sources.

"BAL LINE"

Balanced line inputs, when connected to balanced outputs, offer greater degrees of protection from hum and noise. Some of them have three-pin XLR connectors, but the majority these days tend to have stereo 1/4-inch jack sockets. In this case you use balanced shielded cables which are outwardly similar to regular shielded patch cords, but the wire contains two centre leads plus shielding and the 1/4-inch plugs will be stereo, i.e. with two insulator bands near the tip rather than one. The standard lead designation is tip=in phase, ring=reverse phase, sheild=ground (although there may be a few exceptions). XLR-type balanced patch cords – mic cables can be used for this – are usually designated pin 1=ground, pin 2=in phase, pin 3=reverse phase. It's worth noting that, in a situation where the output is unbalanced but the input is balanced, a regular patch cord will usually work (ditto the reverse situation). Additionally, Audiopro AP-series mixers feature special balancing circuitry which provides the noise rejection of a totally balanced circuit even when the signal source's line output is unbalanced. Simply use a balanced patch cable.

"INSERT"

The insert jack is usually found among the channel input connectors and sometimes among the main and monitor outputs. It is a 1/4-inch stereo jack socket which is actually two jacks in one – a send and a return. This unusual setup is used in place of two separate jacks to save space (some mixers have separate send & return Insert jacks). Using a special "Y" cable with a stereo 1/4-inch plug branching out to two mono 1/4-inch plugs (e.g. Yorkville model PC-6ISPH), you can patch a graphic EQ, compressor/limiter, aural exciter, digital delay, etc. directly into a channel or main/monitor buss. In some cases, the patch cable wiring code is tip=return, ring=send, sleeve=ground, while in others, the wiring goes tip=send, ring=return, sleeve=ground. Check your owner's manual to find out which one your mixer uses. In most mixers, the "send" part of the Insert jack is buffered – in other words, regulated by the channel Gain control. If your wiring is like the first example with the tip being "send", this means that a second mixer, perhaps for monitors, recording or broadcast, can be added on, channel-for-channel, assuming the Insert jacks are not being used for patching purposes. You would simply run shielded, unbalanced patch cords from the Insert jacks to the Line inputs on the other mixer.

"AUX"

Located in the master section, the Auxiliary inputs are always line level and often in stereo pairs, but may or may not be balanced depending on the mixer (AP mixer aux. inputs are stereo, unbalanced). The mixer will usually have an "aux." control in the master section to regulate this input and the signal's final destination will be the "main' mixer channel or one of the "sub" master channels. The purpose of an "aux." input is to permit connecting an additional signal source – perhaps a small outboard mixer for keyboards or drums – without using up one or two input channels.

"EFX RETURN" or "STEREO RETURN"

The effects or stereo return jacks are usually employed as part of the effects "loops". They accept the output of external units – reverb, delay, etc. – and feed it to the mixer's master RETURN controls which regulate its passage to the next master mixer stage. Effects return jacks are usually unbalanced 1/4-inch jack sockets. On stereo mixers, they would be in left/right pairs in order to accept the output of stereo effects units. Alternatively, these can be used as stereo auxiliary inputs, perhaps for connecting a keyboard mixer. The main reason for having multiple EFX or Stereo Return input facilities is to permit you to employ multiple effects "systems", one for each group of input channels. You could, for instance, have echo on the vocals but only reverb on the rest of the band (echo on everything can get too 'muddy' sounding at high volumes.

"AMP IN" or "PA IN"

Powered mixers often have a direct input to the built-in power amp. This is a special 1/4-inch jack socket with a built-in switch that interrupts the flow of all the internal mixer signals to the power amp as soon as you plug into it. Now only the signals which are coming in through the Amp or PA In jack can be amplified. This means that, if you are using an external power amp to drive the Front-Of-House (i.e. main) speaker system, you can patch the mixer's Monitor output into the Amp/PA In jack and simply connect your monitors to the powered mixer's speaker outputs.

"TAPE IN"

Tape inputs are most often RCA ("phono") connectors and basically represent the same thing as "Aux." inputs. They are usually found among the Main, Monitor, Sub, etc. connectors and will have a Tape In level control among the masters.

"TALKBACK"

Some mixers feature a very simple channel consisting of a mic input, a level control, possibly an on/off utton, and a line-level output. This is included to enable the mixing technician to address the lighting technician, a stage hand or road manager through a small amp/speaker system. Some mixers may have the ability to also send some of this signal to one or more of the Aux./ Monitor busses so that the performers may be addressed through the stage monitors. The Talkback input is normally a standard, female XLR mic connector.

THE MIXER - OUTPUTS:

"MAIN", "SUM" or "MONO"

The main, sum or mono output represents a mono signal, usually with its own master and is normally a balanced output (see INPUTS "BAL LINE" for cable wiring). On stereo or multi-buss mixers, it represents the sum of the "Sub" or "Group" buss outputs – in other words, part of the output signal from each Sub or Group buss (channel) goes to the Main, Sum or Mono buss and gets mixed (summed) with the others. In older mono mixers, the Main output is exactly what the name implies and would be connected to the main PA amp/speaker system. In stereo mixers, it can be used for a variety of purposes including main PA, or it can be connected to a remote amp and speaker system, perhaps for the control booth or for recording purposes (remember to split the signal with a "Y" adapter to get it on both tape tracks).

If you have a stereo or multi-buss mixer, one of the possible uses for a Main, Sum or Mono output is to feed the main F.O.H. (front-of- house) amp/speaker system. Since stereo separation does not work as well for PA as it does at home (people at the sides of the stage may end up hearing only guitar and no vocals, etc.), a mono main mix can work as well or better than stereo in some places. If you do decide to go with a mono F.O.H. PA, the "Sub" or "Group" channels can be used as submixes – say, Sub 1 for drums and Sub 2 for the rest of the band in a stereo mixer. The various drum channels' Pan controls would simply be turned all the way Left, for example, and the rest turned Right. Now the Sub or Group One master would regulate all the drum mics at once and the Sub or Group Two master would regulate the rest of the band. The Main, Mono or Sum Master would now regulate the overall level through the PA. In a multi-buss mixer there would, of course, be more submix possibilities. As an example, a four-buss board could accommodate separate vocal, drum and keyboard submixes plus one for the rest of the band.

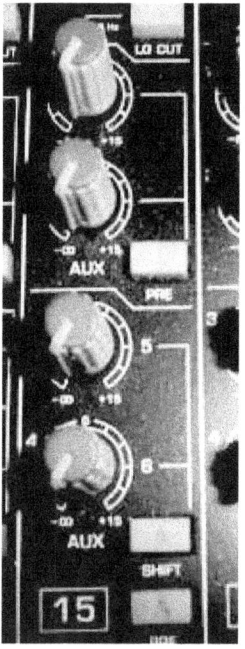

'Sends' - The Mixer Outputs

"SUB or GROUP"

The submix or group outputs are regulated by their own, similarly numbered masters. Stereo mixers have two which would be used to feed a stereo F.O.H. amp/speaker system and they are balanced as a rule (see INPUTS "BAL. LINE for cable wiring). In a multi-buss mixer where there are more than two sub/group channels, these outputs are often used in conjunction with Sub or Group In jacks to create loops with EQ's, compressor/limiters, effects units, etc. which would be dedicated to the needs of the vocals,
instruments or program sources being sent to each buss.(Use of the word 'channel' can get confusing when discussing mixers, therefore in this writing it will be reserved for the input channels only. "Buss" is being used here to represent any mixer circuit which receives signals from the input channels. Expect to see more terms such as "effects buss", "monitor buss", "main buss", etc.).

"MON"

The monitor outputs, like the Main and Sub/Group outs, are usually balanced (see INPUTS "BAL LINE" for cable wiring) and have their own masters. These would be connected to the monitor amp/speaker system. Alternatively, one of the monitor outputs could be connected to the Aux. or Line inputs of a cassette deck with a "Y" adapter so that the signal gets onto both tape tracks. Now the channel Mon.send controls and Monitor master can be used to provide a recording mix while the rest of the board is being used for PA. Tape or Aux. inputs can be used to connect the outputs of the deck to the mixer for playback listening.

"AUX"

The auxiliary outputs are also usually balanced (see INPUTS "BAL LINE" for cable wiring) and, like the others mentioned above, have their own masters. As a rule, they are connected to monitor amp/speaker systems, in fact mixers with full Aux. facilities may not have "monitor" facilities at all. And, like a Mono output, one of the Aux. outputs can be used for recording (see above). Also, by combining them with Aux.In jacks, you can create separate "loops" with EQ's, compressor/limiters or other signal processing units which will now be dedicated to those channels being sent to each Aux. Buss.

"TAPE"

The tape outputs are usually RCA (phono) type and are not balanced. A Tape Send or Tape Out control may be among the masters to regulate the level. If there is no such control, check the owner's manual; chances are the Main or Sub stereo masters control them. If the Tape outputs on your mixer don't have their own master, they're most likely just wired in parallel with the Main or stereo Sub outputs and are regulated by those masters which means that any FOH-system level changes will be reflected in the recording levels. You might want to have someone watch the tape deck's meters and counter adjust its record level control(s). An alternative might be to connect a compressor/limiter (e.g., ART's model SC-2) between the Tape outs and the deck's inputs and set it for "soft knee" compression. Now it will act rather like an automatic volume controller.

"EFX SEND"

The effects send jack is almost always 1/4-inch and may be balanced or unbalanced – check the manual to be sure, however remember that a regular (unbalanced) shielded patch cord will almost always work with a balanced output or input, you simply won't get the extra hum & noise cancellation that balancing provides (you may not hear the difference). Do not connect equalizers, compressors or crossovers to the EFX SEND jack. The effects buss in any mixer is always in parallel with the main busses, not in series with them. As a result, only half of the signals go out through the loop, the rest going straight to the main busses. What finally comes out is a mix of straight and effects-signals. While this is ideal for reverb or echo, you need to put 100% of the signal through EQ's, compressors, etc. For more information, see under "Processors".

"TALKBACK"

This is the output of the Talkback channel. It will be Line level and may be balanced. See under "Mixer Inputs" for more details.

THE MIXER - CONTROLS:

For the sake of clarity, channel controls will be covered from the top to the bottom of the input strip. This is also appropriate because signal flow through the channel circuitry is from top to bottom. (On "box"- style mixer/amplifiers, this is usually reversed because the inputs are at the bottom of the mixer panel).

INPUT CHANNELS -

"GAIN", "TRIM", "ATTEN" or "PAD"

All sources put out different amounts of signal. Some may be weak and others quite strong. It is thus important in larger mixers to be able to adjust the amount of source signal entering the channel. If there is too much, as stated earlier, distortion will result. On the other hand, if there is too little, the channel Level may have to be set much higher than the rest of the channels and the signal-to-noise ratio on that channel will be less than ideal.

About "signal-to-noise" – all audio circuits, even in the most expensive mixers, have a certain level of ambient noise caused by electro-magnetic emanations from all the wiring and equipment nearby. This noise gets amplified along with everything else in a mixer. If the signal is very weak, the channel Level will have to be increased more than the others thus amplifying the noise so that it ends up competing with the signal instead of being drowned out by it. Ideally, the signal should always be much greater than the noise, hence the Gain control is equally as valuable for boosting a weak input signal up to the proper level as it is for reducing the input signal when it's too strong.

At the top of the channel strip, some mixers will have a switch marked "- #dB" (minus some number of decibels) or "Pad". This also is included to help you adjust the input sensitivity for the source signal. The switch will create a very large difference in the signal level corresponding, for example, to the huge difference in signal output between mics and CD players. The Gain or Trim control provides more of a fine-tune capability in accomplishing this task. A few of the more recent mixers only have a Gain or Trim control, no switch. This is possible because active circuitry replaces the input transformers and, as a result, they have such large amounts input headroom and Gain control range that a "pad" is not necessary. One way or another, the channel Clip indicator should be your guide to setting the Gain/Trim/Atten./Pad. While a signal is applied to the input, increase the setting of this feature until the Clip LED flashes, then decrease it slightly.

"CLIP"

In the absence of a channel VU meter, the input clipping indicator is your best aid for setting the Gain/Trim/Pad. This LED is designed to illuminate when the input signal is approaching the upper limit of the input circuit's capacity, but still leaving around 3dB of headroom in most cases (check the manual to be sure). It is thus possible to set the Gain controls simply by watching the channel Clip indicators during a soundcheck and adjusting them for slight amounts of activity.

"MON." or "AUX."

Depending on the mixer design, the Monitor and/or Auxiliary send controls may come next. On mixers with "Pre/Post" EQ selector buttons for these controls, they will come after the EQ section, otherwise they will be right after the Gain, Trim, etc. In order to avoid confusion about how "send" controls work, here is a brief explanation; each channel is capable of sending some of its signal via the internal circuitry to various locations (busses) within the master section. In order to do this there needs to be channel controls to regulate the amount of signal going to each buss. It is not always ideal to have these signals affected by the channel EQ controls since that EQ is there primarily for regulating each channel's sound through the main PA which has different frequency response than the monitor amp/speaker system. The stage monitors operate in a terribly demanding acoustic environment – speakers are close to mics and everything tends to be very loud. As a result, the best way to mix for monitors is to treat them as a totally independent system. Large concert PA's usually have a separate monitor mixer and someone to run it. Smaller systems still need to treat the monitor mix as separately from the main mix as possible. That is why the channel signals would not, as a rule, be EQ'd before being sent to the Mon/Aux. busses. That way, the only equalization they get will be specifically for the stage monitor system. The reason for there being more than one Mon. or Aux. send control on the channel and more than one Mon. or Aux. buss is so that you can mix for more than one monitor system. The drummer, for example, usually needs to hear himself and the vocals extra loudly, and the vocalists, of course, need to hear themselves very loudly while the guitarist might want to hear a predominance of bass and keyboards because his amp is almost all he can hear.

"EQ"

As stated above, the channel equalization is usually desirable only on that portion of the channel signal headed for the FOH system. This is based on the assumption however, that you are using the channel EQ to improve the sound or to get around feedback problems which are exclusive to the FOH PA – not always the case. Some source signals require basic EQ adjustments to sound "right" whether it's through the mains, monitors, on tape or for broadcast. Harmonica mics, for instance, have to be EQ'd to minimize lowfrequency puffing and thumping sounds as well as feedback. For that reason, some mixers have Aux. or Mon. send controls after the EQ with "Pre/Post" selector buttons to put the desired ones through the channel EQ ("Post") or to bypass it ("Pre"). In other mixers, one or more of the Mon/Aux. controls may simply be after the EQ (i.e. "post EQ") and are therefore permanently affected by it. All EQ's function by altering the gain above or below normal over various frequency ranges. As a result, when it comes to setting the channel EQ – or any EQ – there's a golden rule which says "NEVER OVER-EQUALIZE". This is worth remembering because the way you 'think' things should sound and the way they really should sound to ensure that the system works properly all night are not always the same. If the main speaker system has fairly linear frequency response, resist the temptation to "sweeten" the sound, it could save you headaches later on when the SPL (sound pressure level) eventually goes up and the room acoustics begin changing – more about that later. Some mixers offer "semi-parametric" EQ. This usually comes in the form of one or more cut/boost controls, each with a frequency control to position the cut/boost exactly where you want it along the frequency spectrum. One application of such a feature is in the fight against feedback. Here you would turn the cut/boost control counter-clockwise to produce a "dip" in the frequency response, then rotate the frequency control until the dip reaches the guilty frequency and the feedback is reduced.

EQ "SWEEP" Control

Although frequency "sweep" controls have graced the channel EQs of recording mixers for many years, they are only found on the more upscale PA mixers. As a result many PA users, even veterans, are unfamiliar with their function. The SWEEP control determines what range of frequencies is affected by the MID cut/boost. It moves or "sweeps" the MID control's peak or notch in response all the way up to several thousand Hz or down to below one hundred Hz. As a result it can have quite a noticeable effect on the sound especially since the MID cut or boost will be interacting with whatever cuts or boosts you may have set with the LOW or HIGH EQ controls. If you have set a LOW boost, a MID boost swept all the way down to the lowest frequency setting will alter the sound of lows AND increase their volume. Be careful this doesn't damage your woofers and watch out for your tweeters/horns if you sweep the boost up to the higher settings while the HI EQ is boosted. Considering that the SWEEP control can alter everything you are accustomed to an EQ doing, it would be worthwhile to spend some time becoming aquainted with how it works. As music plays through a channel on the mixer and speakers, adjust that channel's MID, first for a boost then for a cut and SWEEP them back and forth. (If there is no MID cut or boost setting, i.e. if it is set at the centre position, the SWEEP will have no effect at all). Now repeat the process with that channel's LOW and HIGH EQ controls at various settings but with the volume at a safe level for the speakers. Together, MID and SWEEP controls can be used to accomplish a variety of tasks from combating feedback to improving the way things sound through the PA or on recording. Here are some of those tasks & settings:

• Killing feedback; set MID at −6dB and slowly rotate SWEEP until the feedback stops. If needed cut Mid further.

• "Bonky" sounding snare drum; −6dB @ 200Hz (and roll off LOW EQ −6dB)

• "Boomy" bass drum; −6dB @ 300Hz (with LOW EQ at +6dB & HIGH EQ at +3dB)

· "Fwashy" sounding cymbals. −9dB @ 300Hz (roll off LOW EQ −15dB)

· Excessive hiss from guitar, bass or keyboard amp; +3dB @ 5kHz (with HI EQ rolled off −9dB)

· Fading vocal range (notes too low for singer); +3dB @ 80Hz (with LOW EQ rolled off −6dB)

• "Puffing" on harmonica mic; −9dB @ 80Hz (with LOW EQ rolled off −12dB)

• Rack Toms; −3dB @400 Hz

• Floor tom; −6dB @ 200Hz

{Note: These are **approximate** settings only. Use them as a starting point and "tune around" them. Generally speaking, you will probably end up with the MID in cut mode for most problem-solving uses of the SWEEP control. In any case you will learn to use this feature judiciously. The best PA EQ setting is the one with the LEAST adjustment, but when you need to solve a problem it's good to know how to use the tools.

"EFX"

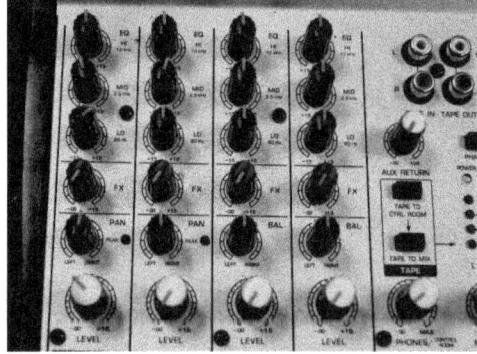

Unlike the MON/AUX send controls, the effects send controls are always post-EQ and post-fader, i.e. They are affected by both the channel equalization and the channel fader (in PA vernacular they are "postpost"). There may be more than one EFX send control and they may feed either an internal effects circuit (reverb) or a master Effects Send buss, check the owner's manual if there is more than one EFX control on each channel to see which one is which. In any case, the channel EFX signals are internally routed to their designated master effects summing busses where they are mixed together on their way to the EFX SEND jack or internal effect.

When mixing effects such as reverb or echo, don't overdo it. Most halls, clubs, etc. have at least some natural reverberation and the sound can become ill-defined or "mushy" if just a little too much reverb/echo is applied. In places with an audible echo, no matter how short the duration, you are probably better off not to use any reverb/echo at all.

"PAN"

The Pan control, found only on mixers with stereo Main outputs, functions a bit like the "balance" control on a home stereo system. In fact it regulates how much of the channel's post-EQ signal gets routed to either the Left or Right Main PA busses. If, for example, the Pan control is rotated all the way left, that channel's signal will only go to the left Main buss. If the F.O.H. (main) PA is stereo, only the speakers on the left side of the stage will be producing that channel's output − not an ideal situation.

In most PA situations, the only real reason for running a stereo F.O.H. system is to get the sonic benefit of a stereo reverb. When you consider that the natural hall reverb is likely to muddy this effect and you aren't likely to be using a lot of reverb anyway, you have to wonder what the PAN controls are good for, other than certain recording applications, e.g.. "positioning" certain sources in the soundfield . However, if you have a basic stereo mixer with a "Main" master and corresponding mono output, and you are running a mono F.O.H. system, the PAN controls can be used to establish two main mixdowns, perhaps one for drums and the other for the rest of the band. With the drum channels panned left (for instance) and all the rest panned right, the Left submaster fader now becomes the drum submaster, the other becomes the band master and your mono Main fader regulates overall level.

"PFL" or "CUE"

The Pre-Fade Listen or Cue button sends post-EQ channel signal to the headphone amplifier so that individual channels can be isolated through the phones. Because the PFL/Cue signal is tapped off just before the channel fader (hence "pre-fade") you can shut that channel down through the FOH PA, but still hear it through your headphones. This is a convenient feature for previewing channels before bringing them into the mix (e.g.., for cueing tapes up). It may also be used for checking out problems – a squealing amp, a distorted mic, etc.

"MUTE"

The Mute button is usually inserted just after the EQ section. We mention it at the end of the channel section simply because that is where the button most often appears – i.e. conveniently close to the channel fader and PFL/Cue button. As the name implies it silences the channel through the FOH system and possibly the monitors (check your manual). Its prime function is to enable the user to pre-set a channel's level, EQ, Efx sends and Mon./Aux. sends then shut the channel off to be added to the music program later on. Muting is a convenient feature for infrequently-used channels such as harmonica mic, acoustic guitar, banjo, mandolin, certain wind and percussion instruments, pre-recorded music or sound effects, all of which should be left off when not in use to reduce unwanted sound pickup and the risk of feedback. The Mute button is often used as a quick first step to getting rid of a problem. If a mic is feeding back for instance, you can Mute it then EQ the feedback on that channel (see >>EQ above) or have someone move the offending mic, then lower the channel fader level, take the channel off Mute and bring the fader level back up. Of course, if muting the channel does not cure the feedback, either the monitor is feeding back or you have the wrong channel. Turn down the Monitor control and if that doesn't work, return that channel to normal status and try muting the next most suspicious one (nobody said pro sound was going to be easy).

"PHASE" or "POLARITY"

The input phase or polarity reversal button may appear at the bottom or top of the channel. As the name implies, it flips the polarity of the input signal so that it is 180 degrees out of phase with the other channels. This feature is most commonly used to combat certain persistent feedback problems where two mics are picking up the same source and feeding it to a nearby speaker, usually a monitor.

"L-R", "1-2", "3-4", etc.

Multi-buss mixers often feature pushbuttons on the channels which direct the post-fader, post-pan channel output to selected "pairs" of Main mix busses. That way, you may employ the stereo submixing section of your choice and Pan between its two masters.
Remember to de-select one pair of submasters when changing to another to avoid gain buildup and feedback.

MASTER SECTION CONTROLS:

The masters generally act as output level controls for their designated output connectors, one exception being the EFX or STEREO RETURN master(s) since those jacks are inputs. Aside from that, everything does exactly what its name implies. See under MIXER OUTPUTS for further information on any of these features.

"MAIN"

This master regulates the output of the MAIN, SUM or MONO buss where the outputs of the SUB or GROUP busses or Left & Right stereo master busses get mixed down into a single signal.

"SUB" or "GROUP"

These masters regulate the SUBmix or GROUP output levels.

"MON"," AUX" or "EFX"

These masters regulate the output level of their designated SEND or OUT jacks.

"RTN"

These masters regulate the input levels of their designated RETURN jacks.

"EFX TO MAIN/EFX TO MON"

Some mixers with effects busses feature controls which are actually effects return masters, but one sends the effects signal to the input of the main busses and the other to the input of the monitor buss. In either case, the effects signal gets mixed with the straight signals coming directly from the channels (yes, electrons actually travel fast enough for some of them to leave the mixer via the Efx Send jack, go through perhaps several cables and effects devices, come back in through the Efx Return jack and still arrive inside the mixer at the input of the main or monitor buss circuits at the same time as internal signals direct from the channels .

"PAN"

These controls pan the Stereo Return signals between pairs of SUB or GROUP masters.

"TAPE" or "2-TRACK"

This regulates the level of the Tape or 2-Track outputs.

"TALKBACK"

This regulates the level of the Talkback output.

"EQ"

A graphic equalizer is featured on some mixers and a few have more than one, in which case one of the graphics will usually be for the monitor buss. As mentioned earlier, equalizers work by increasing or decreasing the signal strength (a.k.a. "gain") over various narrow bands of frequencies. As a result they are equally capable of curing or causing problems and should be treated with care. To get rid of feedback, pull the EQ faders down one at a time, remembering to push them back up to centre if the feedback doesn't stop. Eventually you should find the one which reduces or stops the feedback. If possible, adjust it back up slightly so that the gain isn't overly reduced. As always, the golden rule is NEVER OVER-EQUALIZE. If there is a persistent feedback problem requiring large cuts in the EQ settings, move the mic or the speaker to get rid of it. EQ cuts cost the system valuable decibels of sound pressure. If the mic or speaker can't be moved, the next best solution is to ascertain which channel has the problem then insert an external EQ directly into the that channel (see "Insert" under Inputs). This way the necessary EQ cuts will only affect whichever channel has the problem, not the whole system. The process of "sweetening" the FOH system· fs sound with low and high-frequency EQ boosts should be done with great care in live music applications. Keep them to a maximum of 3dB (preferably less). For DJ applications this is less of a stringent limitation, but boosts of more than
6dB should be avoided. And when in doubt, LEAVE THE FADERS AT CENTRE – there's no shame in a "flat" EQ; quite often it's the sign of a good system and a wise technician.

You're looking at the desk, a bewildering melange of knobs and sliders with strange, alien names. You ask...

"Terms like 'Gain', and 'Trim' – What's that all about?"
The signals (noises) coming into the desk are at different levels – if a signal exceeds the level which the mixer circuitry can cope with it will be distorted, if it is too far below that level it will require amplification to bring it up. The 'gain' control determines the amount of amplification applied a signal. The simplest way of setting 'gain trim' is to set the *channel* and *output* faders (all these terms are explained below) at their *unity gain* position – the odB mark, about 3/4 of the way up the scale, and then input the loudest signal you're likely to encounter. Adjust the gain trim so that the signal is just going into the red (check on the visual metering).

"Phantom Power?"

A desk may allow 'phantom power' to be selected individually for each channel or it may be a universal 'on or off' decision for entire desk. Knowing which is the case is important. Phantom Power is a 48v supply drawn from the mixer and available to channels fed by kit that requires a separate power supply for inbuilt pre-amp circuits – essentially this will be any Condenser type microphones (but not Dynamic mics) and some active DI boxes. As a general rule, keep Phantom Power 'off' unless it is actually required. If the Phantom Power supply is 'global' there is no problem having it on to power a DI Box or Condenser Mic provided that all Dynamic Mics (the 'standard' type of mic such as Shure 57s & 58s) are connected with *balanced* cables. If the connector is of the three pin XLR type it is a balanced cable.

"What is a Channel?"
A channel is an audio input that goes to a fader. A typical mixer channel will have an input selector for choosing mic or line signals, a trim knob for adjusting the input level, and dedicated EQ (equalization) controls to alter the bass, midrange and treble bands of the signal. A channel usually has sends which send part of the signal to an effects unit (or other destination). Finally a channel may have a bus selector switch (the routing buttons we saw before), which switches the channel output to a *bus.*

"What's a Bus?"
A bus is a fader with its own dedicated output. You could also say that a bus is a major pathway from all channels to a single fader connected to an output. You can send everything going to that fader out of the mixer to another piece of gear - You can also bring the signal back in to the mixer on spare channels. Why would you want to do this? External FX processing for example. On mixers with busses, there are routing buttons (see below) on each channel that lets you route the whole signal to one of the busses. The Main bus is often called the L/R bus. Other busses are often grouped in pairs, like the 1-2 bus, 3-4 bus, (see routing buttons below) - pay attention, there'll be questions later! There may also be another switch that lets you route these bus faders to the Master fader.

Typical uses of busses are to send a track (or groups of tracks) to a digital multitrack, or to a soundcard or audio interface. Yet you can also be very creative with them, such as sending them to samplers, grooveboxes with analog inputs, surround encoders, separate compressors etc. Some busses may have *inserts*. These let you return the external signal to the mixer without using more *channels*.

"What is a channel insert? "
An insert is a pathway out and then back again into a single fader. You use it to patch in an external piece of gear that only affects that one channel. Typical uses of inserts are patching compressors, outboard EQs, exciters, pedals, multi-track recorder input/outputs, and FX boxes. Lots of people route channel inserts to a patchbay where they can plug in various devices conveniently. Hardware plugins. On a well featured mixer, there are inserts on individual channels, busses and the master *fader*.

"What is a fader? "
A fader is a sliding level control that can be used to vary the loudness of any mixer channel. The name comes from "fading in" and "fading out" tracks. Is there a little "infinity" symbol at the bottom? Infinity means "zero" in mixer-speak. See the heavy line next to the solo button? That is the marker for 0dbvu, sometimes called the "nominal" or normal level. It signifies that at that point the signal that exits the fader is the same as the signal that entered the fader. If you lower the fader from that point you attenuate (ie reduce) the signal. If you raise the fader from that point you add gain to (or boost) the signal.

"What is a pan pot?"
A pan pot, is a little knob marked 'pan' - it is, of course, a "panoramic potentiometer" but if you know that then you're err - well, not reading this I guess.... A pan pot allows you to place the signal it applies to (see 'channel') anywhere in the stereo field, from extreme left to extreme right and all stops in between. It helps you separate the sounds in the mix - very handy when you find yourself with flute, sax and harmonica playing guests.

"What are the mute/solo buttons?"
The mute button silences the audio on a channel (so you can hear other stuff in the mix). A solo button silences everything except the signal on a channel so you can hear that channel in isolation. Our (un)sound engineer will

always mute a channel not currently being used (lest someone inadvertently wreck his mix by coughing on a live mic or smacking a guitar into a mic stand? Yes, but more so because an 'open' mic is an invitation to feedback.

"What are routing buttons? "

Switches that switch the audio signal down the pathway to the busses. You might think of them as an output selector for now. If you press the 3-4 button and pan all the way left, the signal goes out bus out 3. If you press the 1-2 button and pan all the way right, the signal only goes out bus 2. If you press 1-2, 3-4, and L-R and pan center the signal goes out all 6 outputs. I recommend you try all these options just to know what the results are - we had the desk for 6 months before we realised how useful this could be.

"What's a Send and Return? "

A send is a major audio path that goes out of the mixer. On each channel there is (usually) a knob for each send so you can direct variable amounts of that channel to the pathway. This can function as a separate monitor mix. In a recording situation, the send typically goes to an FX unit. The 4 turquoise knobs in the photo (right) are sends. The signal is brought back to the mixer by the returns, and can be added to the main signal. A send is effectively a submix. You don't have to bring back the sends to their returns. You can bring them back to an empty channel and continue to process with EQ, or on to a bus fader. You can use the returns like any other line input, patching in synths, other mixers, computer soundcards, a cd player, decks and anything else you can think of.

"Can you use a live console/mixer for recording to your DAW? "

A DAW is a digital audio workstation such as your pc or mac. You know it's a yes, I already told you! Use the busses to get an isolated signal to your DAW, sound-card, or audio interface. They all work the same way. Or use the inserts to connect to the DAW with unbalanced cables (your mixer manual will explain these). Shut off the global EQ. Things to look for - focus on whether the mixer has all the ins and outs you need. Does it have enough busses? Do you need direct outs? How many sends and returns, preamps do you need? How is phantom power implemented? Are all the connections balanced (see balanced/unbalanced below)? Which are not? This is a recording issue and beyond the scope of this little book but any good home recording guide will give you the information you need. 90% of the digital mixers now available will do the job well - the size of the mixer, in terms of the number of inputs, is likely to be the variable factor but how many channels will you need to record at once?

"How Big a Desk Do We Need for our Live Work?"

The number of inputs is the issue but note that 24 channels may only give you 12 analogue inputs and those are the ones you need for your mic's and any DIs. Bear in mind that if you are mic'ing drums that could be 3 to 5 mic inputs or more. Behringer typically indicate the spec in the model name - the Xenyx 2222 has a USB interface (the Xenyx bit), 22 channels, 2 busses and 2 master outs. The 2442 has 24 channels, 4 busses and 2 master outs. The former gives you 10 analogue inputs, the latter 12. Not all manufacturers use such descriptive model names however.

"What's this Balanced and Unbalanced stuff about?"

The XLR (mic') lead is balanced, similarly speaker leaders, and the guitar/instrument lead is unbalanced. Three wire system, balanced, and two wire system, unbalanced. In the balanced lead the positive and the negative don't contact the earth whereas in the unbalanced lead the negative and the earth are one and the same thing. The earth - (ground) is exactly that. The green earth wire goes to a copper stake in the ground so that any short circuit between the positive and earth will send the current to ground. But because the positive and the negative don't contact the earth it is said to be floating 'above ground'. The shield acts as a protection from interference by sending any extraneous electrical interference like hum, to ground. Unfortunately in the *unbalanced* circuit negative is ground! This makes your choice of stage box (multicore cable) important as good ones feature a built-in 'ground-lift' that cancels that irritating hum which can drive sound engineers to distraction.

Unbalanced

The two signals of an unbalanced connection are referred to as "signal" and "ground". The ground is the zero reference while the signal has a voltage level that is above or below zero. This voltage level determines whether the signal is a 1 or a 0 (VGA, Audio & Video are Analog signals, the analog signal can have a voltage level anywhere between the high and low voltage levels). Coax cabling reduces exposure to cross-talk.
Balanced

Balanced signals are often called "current loop" signals and travel on "twisted pairs" (UTP for Unshielded Twisted Pair or STP for Shielded Twisted Pair). The two signals in a balanced pair are like opposite charges of each other. What that means is if one wire has 12 volts, the other wire will have -12 volts. As the signal travels the pair, one wire radiates a magnetic field but as its partner wire generates an opposite field, the two fields cancel out. This cancelling is how signals eliminate 'cross-talk'. Since Twisted pair wire is usually cheaper then Coax wire, balanced signals are more popular.

Make sure that you have the appropriate cables and always have back-up. As with so many things in your live set-up, the cheap buy often turns out to be the most expensive over a period of time but a misplaced Doc Marten can swiftly kill the best shielded cable...

Getting Started – What Do You Need?

What you will need to accomplish is the key:

1. You need to deliver your sound to the audience
2. You need to be able to hear yourself

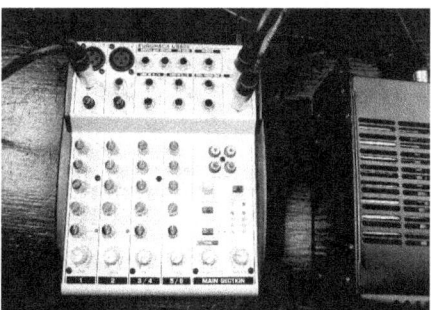

You'd think that a band, with amps and a drummer, will make such a noise that both these objectives are a given but it's just not so. You'll hear a lot of *noise* and so will the audience but on neither count will it be the SOUND that you want. And the same applies to the solo performer with a guitar, once you move beyond the confines of a living room or campfire whole new dynamics come into play.

You will need a PA – this can be a basic, starter kit – I recommend a powered mixer and a couple of good full range speakers. While it is true that many venues will have a PA not many will provide you with monitors, so a good starter kit would be a **powered mixer** and three or four **wedge type full range speakers**. This will give you a rehearsal PA with plenty of inputs and simple, easy to use FX. It can act as your monitor system for gigs. Add a couple of **DI boxes** and you'll have a back-up in the event of amp failure or power amp/main PA breakdowns too. Does this happen? Yes. Often.

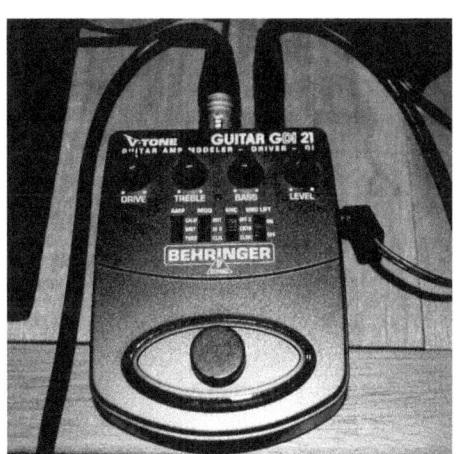

You will also need **microphones**. Don't stop at the vocalist or the backing vocalist, think about how you are going to collect the guitar and bass sounds from the back-line amps if these are to go through the front of house PA system, and think about the drums, too. For small, first gigs you can manage without mic'ing guitar amps and you'll probably get by with just the kick drum mic'd, or perhaps an overhead for the drums. Basic SM57 type dynamic mics will get you started and for most on-stage needs are all you'll ever need but you can explore condenser and ribbon microphones when the band's earnings warrant it! The microphones will need **mic stands** and make sure these have **mic holders** that fit your mic's.

And cables... **balanced cables** for each microphone, work on two for each mic. **Speaker cable** for the monitors – label it so it doesn't get mixed up with instrument cables. I recommend getting a multi-core (aka 'python' or 'snake') as it simplifies and tidies everything, makes setting up much easier and faster. Everything plugs into one stage box and is then trunked by a single cable to the mixer where it branches out into individual cables again. The multi-core has sends and returns so can deliver signals from the mixer back to the stage too. They aren't

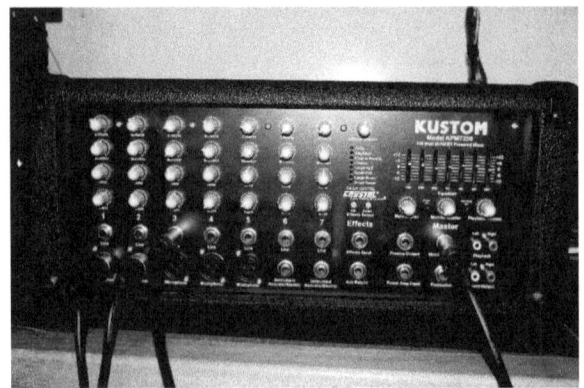

*An inexpensive powered mixer like this is a great starter -
good for rehearsing and monitors.*

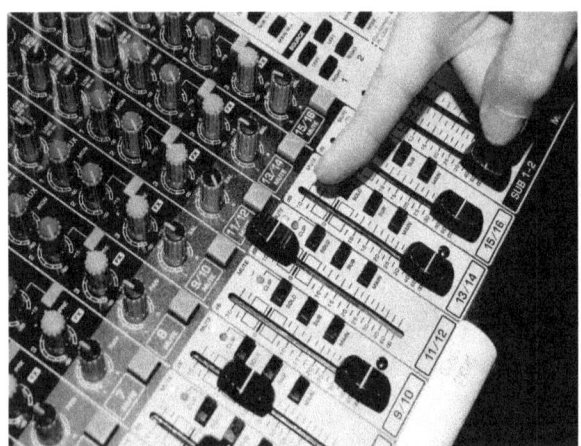

*A medium sized portable mixing desk will handle a typi-
cal start-up band's input requirements - our desk had 22
inputs, 3 aux sends per channel - we used everything!
Don't scrimp, get the biggest you can.*

cheap but they are well worth it and pay for themselves
very quickly through the lack of broken cables – on stage,
cables get trampled, tripped over and ripped out with great
regularity – not so a single gaffered multi-core. **Gaffer
tape** deserves a mention. Lots of it on the list.

If you're playing on a bill with others, find out what gear
you might be able to share but it's always better to have
your own kit that you're familiar with and the list above is
relatively easy for a band to transport without resorting to
truck hire.

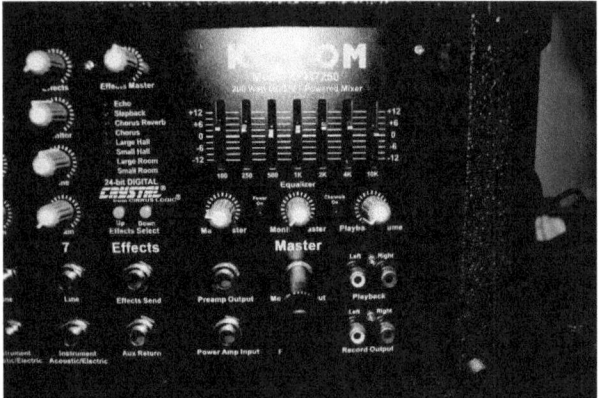

*A closer view of some of the options, and outputs a simple pow-
ered mixer can provide.*

It would be easy to add a chapter to this book recommending what to buy, with pros and cons, reviews… but,
just as this book refuses to tell you how to mix your sound – that's something you need to figure out yourself – it
isn't about to start being specific about one piece of technology over another. Technology is just moving so fast
right now that it would swiftly be out of date. Check my web site and articles for the latest news and views –
http://www.jezrogers.com is a good place to start. See you there!